Sexual intimacy MATTERS

THE ULTIMATE GUIDE FOR WOMEN IN LONG-TERM RELATIONSHIPS

DEAR EM

Printed in the United States of America
First Printing, 2021

Interior Design: Jennie Lyne @bookcoverit.com

ISBN EBook 978-1-7365615-0-8
ISBN Paperback 978-1-7365615-1-5
ISBN Hardback 978-1-7365615-2-2

ALSO BY DEAR EM
My SIM Journal

sexualintimacymatters.com

CONTENTS

KEY TEN:

Hello You, Dear Em Here

I'm so excited you've chosen to explore your *Sexual Intimacy Matters* with me! Before we dive in, let me share a little about myself so you can understand why I felt compelled to write this guide for women. Here's a glimpse into my personality, my connection to sexuality, my relationships, and exactly why I'm on a mission to help women restore the bond of sexual intimacy in their long-term relationships.

As far as personalities go, authenticity is the essence of who I am. I'm a straight shooter who functions best in honesty. I see no point in sugarcoating anything. My life experiences have taught me to be non-judgmental. It's simply not my place to look down my nose at others. Being understanding and highly empathetic gives me a well-rounded perspective on situations, rather than a one-sided view. At first, I'm quiet and reserved, until you get to know me. Then *look out!* I'm a little naughty with a twist of humor. I hope this part of my personality translates well throughout this guide.

Since a core part of my personality is openness, I've always felt comfortable speaking freely about sexuality. Be it playful banter or serious conversation, it's never a subject I shy away from or feel embarrassed to discuss. Since puberty, I've been fortunate enough to feel at ease exploring the world of sexuality. As I've matured into a woman, I've remained connected to this part of myself. I believe sexuality is such a natural and integral part of humanity, and we should feel free to explore it without shame or judgment, but rather with playful curiosity, excitement, and a sense of adventure.

For most of my life, I've been in long-term relationships. Three of four relationships turned into marriage. Now, hold on, I know what you're thinking. "This woman's a serial wife!" No, no! It's really not quite as bad as it seems! Marriage number one was to my first boyfriend, and it ended in divorce just two short years later. My mother, bless her heart, tried to warn me that 20 years old was too young to make that type of commitment, but what did she know? Like most young adults, I thought I knew it all...and then some. I learned after that experience that Mother actually *does* know best! From then on, I listened to her when she felt the need to guide me, and who knew? She offered me some great advice over the years.

Let's move along to my second marriage. John and I spent ten years together. We fell madly in love, got married, had two boys, and built a successful business together. Unfortunately, he passed away from cancer at age 35, leaving me a widow at age 37 with our two young boys. Our world turned upside down during his illness and in the wake of his passing. It was very difficult for us to adjust to this monumental loss. Although I understand no one is promised tomorrow, it still feels like we were all robbed of time. To those fortunate enough to live the full scope of life, I say, *how lucky you are.*

But as the old saying goes...*life goes on*, and it does. I picked up the pieces of my life as best as possible and met my current husband, Angel. We believe it was destiny for our paths to cross, to help each other learn and grow in ways we both needed for personal development. We've been together for 13 years now, and hands down, this relationship has generated the most self-growth for us both. I truly appreciate his candidness about the male perspective and how he openly shares with me the real deal many men go through in long-term relationships. He has a tremendous amount of deep insight and wisdom, which I've learned from him and will share with you.

Based on the mistakes, lessons learned, challenges, and epiphanies I've experienced throughout my relationships, I can now see crystal clear how either the weakened or strong bond of sexual intimacy affected each relationship. If I can share the knowledge I've gained to help even one couple turn their efforts back into their relationship to make it healthy and whole once again, I will consider my mission a success.

So, why is the bond of sexual intimacy in *your* relationship *my* mission? The reason is simple. I believe too many relationships become tainted by avoidable problems, transition into boring living arrangements, or ultimately end because the weakened or broken connection of sexual intimacy has either directly or indirectly impacted the relationship. Although sexual intimacy is only one moving part among many, the sexual bond is firmly attached to all other parts of the relationship. If this bond slips away, it affects the entirety of the relationship. A ripple effect occurs. Many people may not see it that way or understand the reality of that statement, but as you read through this guide, you will understand beyond the shadow of a doubt that it's all connected.

I created this guide with a hard-won understanding of *Sexual Intimacy Matters* and how it affects so many women in long-term relationships. From my heart, I sincerely hope you will take something away from this guide to bring positive change to your relationship. **With open communication, decisive action, and mutual love, any relationship can turn around and become exactly what you and your partner desire.** Although it does take much, much (did I mention MUCH?) more effort to keep things fresh, exciting, solid, and strong in a long-term relationship, it is absolutely possible and definitely worth it.

All my love,

Dear Em

For Your Information

My authority to speak about sexual intimacy matters is supported by certifications in relationship and women's holistic health coaching, coupled with decades of firsthand experience of being in healthy (and not so healthy) long-term relationships. It has been one of my favorite life projects to learn and grow as much as possible within these lesson-filled wonderlands relationships can offer. Deep down, you probably know what you need to do to improve your relationship. However, sometimes you need an outsiders perspective to help bring clarity to the surface.

As you progress through this guide, it's possible you may find some challenging or unfamiliar content due to the sensitive nature of sexual intimacy. Try to keep an open mind about topics that may push the boundaries of your comfort zone. Embrace this guide as an invaluable resource and safe space to help you learn, grow, and become more comfortable with *Sexual Intimacy Matters.*

The information and advice offered in this guide should not take the place of professional counseling. It is simply a resource to help your relationship become happy, healthy, and whole once again.

Lastly, although this guide references the traditional male/female relationship, the information also applies to females in any kind of romantic relationship.

Which Woman Are *You?*

Are you a new mom, exhausted, overwhelmed, and busy juggling all your new responsibilities? Or perhaps you're already a seasoned mother with multiple children, always on call and trying to meet their every need. Whether you're a stay-at-home mom or pulling double duty as a full-time working mother, you can't see straight because you're beyond busy with your endless to-do list. What's the word I'm looking for to describe a typical day in a mother's life? Ah yes...***overloaded!***

Oh, you don't have children that require your attention every waking moment? Then maybe you're a no-nonsense powerhouse in the corporate world. You're all business and keep tenaciously focused on your career. You bring your never-ending workload home and stay immersed in your business affairs long into the night, forgetting much of what or who exists around you. Your partner often expresses how much it affects him that you're physically there yet still absent. You have lost the ability to maintain a healthy balance between work and play, and this imbalance negatively impacts your relationship.

Or perhaps you are a woman who has reached the milestone in life where some thief in the night has robbed your hormones. You feel almost completely void of sexual desire, you often sweat bullets from hot flashes, your vagina has become a desert, and you now have to cross your legs every time you cough, laugh, or sneeze to avoid peeing your pants. Doesn't menopause seem like a cruel payback for being the chosen gender to bring children into the world? After what the female body endures from childbirth alone, we should be rewarded with...I don't know...eternal youth...or spontaneous orgasms...or at a bare minimum, lifetime priority parking at our favorite grocery store, but at least something pleasant...not menopause!

Could it be that you've lost self-confidence as you've aged? Maybe you've had a child or two—or five—and you now have residual physical effects causing you to feel self-conscious. It could be extra weight, stretch marks, or the deflated remains of your once perky boobs from breastfeeding. Maybe all three! As if that weren't bad enough, there's the inexorable progression of aging, including but not limited to wrinkles (no, they are *not* smile lines), a turkey neck, flappy bat-wing arms, cellulite in places you didn't think it could migrate to, kinky gray hairs popping through your luscious locks, a road map of veins slowly spreading across your legs, and your once tiny waist has expanded to the width of your shoulders. *Whaaaat the hell?*

If you haven't experienced the joys (read: miseries) of aging yet, then savor your youth, my spring chicken, for it *will* sneak up on you. All these minor and major physical changes can chip away at your confidence, wreak havoc on your self-esteem, and make you feel insecure about your appearance.

Could you be a woman who has suffered the excruciating pain of infidelity? Maybe you're still in the process of healing this deep wound, which is very delicate and difficult to repair. Choosing to stay with your partner after this massive breach of trust is a long, long road back to recovery. There is a constant inner-battle playing in your mind. The feelings of injustice rage against the desire to trust him again and rebuild a better relationship. You have never felt quite so torn about anything in your whole life, and you can't help but look at him through the eyes of both optimism and skepticism. You wonder if you will be able to reestablish a healthy physical connection after this emotional devastation or if you will ever completely recover from the unbearable pain this betrayal has caused.

Is it possible you feel a sense of hopelessness with your partner? He doesn't seem interested in you anymore, and you feel starved for the attention and affection he once showered upon you. You can't even remember the last time he made a romantic gesture. You have tried and tried to convey your feelings, but to no avail. Living this way makes you feel lonely and hollow. Because of the extreme emptiness, you may have permitted yourself to go outside the boundaries of your relationship to feel desired and appreciated. You so desperately want to experience what you pine for in your relationship, but you don't foresee it happening. Maybe you haven't taken the physical step outside of your relationship yet, but you have contemplated what was once unthinkable and found the thought seriously tempting.

And maybe, just maybe, it's as simple as this: you are amongst the countless number of women who are experiencing feelings of boredom and complacency most women encounter in a long-term relationship. Like a slow-growing waistline, these characteristics tend to creep unnoticed into your relationship. Then *bam!* You wake up and realize the excitement has turned dull, the freshness has grown stale, and the passion has long since faded away. You love your partner and generally feel happy, but frankly, you also feel...eh, *bored*. I hate to say it, but there's a good chance he feels the same way too.

Which one of these women best describes you? Do you fit one category, maybe two, or perhaps more? I've fit into almost all these women's shoes at one point or another. I believe the one common factor that plays a quiet and unassuming yet powerful role in the ultimate success or failure of a long-term relationship is the bond of sexual intimacy. A big and bold statement, I know. But have you ever thought, I mean *really thought* about what a significant role this bond plays in your relationship? Have you considered its connection with all the other working parts of a relationship? For many women, the answer is no. After all, you're too busy trying to keep up with the constant demands of everyday life. Maybe you're vaguely aware, but you put little thought into it because honestly, where would you even begin?

Rest assured, keeping the bond of sexual intimacy strong is a vital factor in maintaining a healthy and well-rounded relationship.

If you don't constantly nurture this aspect of your relationship like a newborn baby, you and your partner can become merely child-rearing partners, companions, friends (or worse, enemies), or roommates. These relationships revolve around living arrangements. You want more than a living arrangement, don't you? You want passion. You want to feel desirable. You want that spark of excitement again because it makes you feel *so alive!*

Is this possible? Is there potential to revitalize your relationship from its current condition? Is it possible to feel passion and desire again for this man you've been with forever and a day? My answer is a resounding YES! Anything is possible if you possess this one critical driving force: **DESIRE.** It's what motivates us to create or change anything we want in our lives. ***Anything!***

So then, are you ready? I mean...are you *really* ready? You are about to embark upon a journey of your inner self and rediscover the amazing benefits that long-term relationships can offer. Bring desire, an open mind, and a sincere willingness, and I'll bring my experience, guidance, and suggestions to turn your desire into reality. Deal?

The Dilemma

What a perfect evening—a romantic dinner by candlelight. You find yourself feeling enraptured and carefree as you savor a soft white wine and enjoy lighthearted, flirtatious conversation. You can't remember the last time you felt so special, so deserving of these showers of loving attention. In a phrase, you feel like a woman. After leaving the quaint beachfront restaurant, you and your dream man meander down a dimly lit path leading to a deserted beach. Along the way, you pause to sit on a weathered wooden bench and take off your heels. As you slip them off, the gentle ocean breeze tousles your hair, and the heavenly feeling of cool, powdery sand envelops your bare feet. A flutter of warmth travels through your body, lands in the center of your heart, and caresses your soul.

The reflection of luminous stars in the glassy low tide catches your eye as you stroll hand-in-hand towards the shoreline. Your gaze turns outward to admire the moonbeams dancing playfully across the endless, shimmering ocean.

You could pinch yourself in disbelief because you cannot believe you are here, on this beautiful beach, in this indelible moment, with this too-good-to-be-true man. He interrupts your thoughts by slipping an arm around your waist. His touch is pure magic. It's been ages since a simple touch made you breathless with excitement. He nudges your hip and pauses, turning your body towards him. Tenderly, he wraps his strong arms around your waist, pulling your body close. His face is intense with sincere adoration, and desire fills his eyes. His gaze alone creates anticipation and excitement deep within you. He brings your hands up to his sexy lips and slowly kisses one then the other. He gracefully sweeps you off your feet and gently lays you on the powdery sand. Propped on an elbow, he positions himself close, leans down, and begins lightly kissing your face, your lips, the nook under your ear, the soft spot beneath your collarbone, and across your whole body. *I can't believe this man is here with me,* you think distractedly to yourself. *He's so romantic, so passionate, so handsome, and his lips...oh his lips feel so amazing!*

Your mind spins in a whirlwind of pleasure, and you're lost in the moment's bliss. He moves one hand along the side of your body, gently tracing his fingers down the outside of your hip and thigh and back up your inner thigh, underneath your dress. He never stops kissing you, making you crazy with desire. His fingers pull aside your panties as he begins softly caressing between your legs. The sensation sends a wave of electricity through your whole body. You haven't been touched with this kind of passion for such a long time. Within moments, you start to feel the intense buildup take hold of your body. You begin the most amazing orgasm and then...

Beep! Beep! Beep!

The obnoxious blaring of your alarm rips you awake smack in the middle of your orgasm, stealing you from the brief ecstasy of your incredible and *oh so realistic* dream. You find your hand between your legs and realize your body subconsciously helped you with a much-needed sexual release.

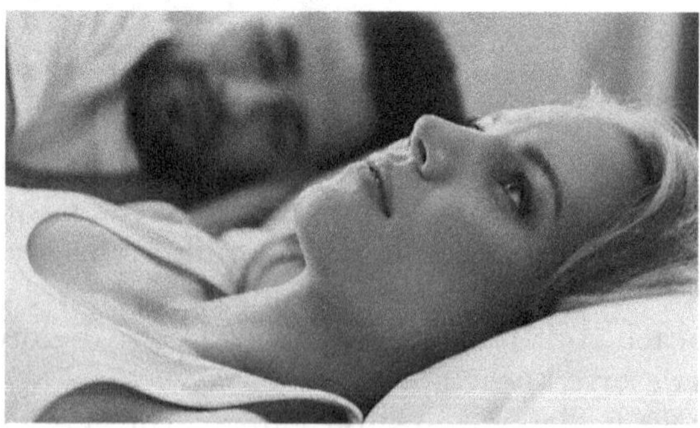

[Note: Wet dreams are a good indicator it's been WAY too long since you've had an orgasm!]

You stretch slowly and lie there for a minute, adjusting yourself to the waking world. The endorphin rush fades too quickly as you relive the dream again and again. You think, *Ugh, it's been way too long since I've felt that surge of excitement.* You glance sideways, hoping you didn't wake your partner while you were in fantasy land. You didn't. He continues to snore through the hush of early morning. You gaze at the ceiling and sigh. All those incredible feelings created by Mr. Tall, Dark and Handsome make you suddenly realize...

Something BIG is missing in your relationship.

You look at him again before rolling out of bed to tackle another crazy day. You ask yourself, *Well damn, when did things change? When was the last time we had sex for more than five minutes or even kissed for that matter? How on earth did our relationship arrive in this barren wasteland? What happened?*

* * *

Has the passion and sexual fire between you, once burning so hot, now grown cold? Or maybe it's still smoldering...but *barely*. Do you feel that your once-strong bond of intimacy has become lost in the jungle of work and/or motherhood? Is romance a ball you dropped while juggling a hundred other responsibilities? Do you crash into bed at night deliriously tired, cursing tomorrow because you know it will be the same grind? Do you secretly wish it would all somehow disappear, if only for a few moments, just long enough to catch your breath?

There's only so much time in a day. In the end, you're just one person being pushed and pulled in so many directions. Something must be sacrificed to maintain an adequate level of sanity. *But what?* Albeit a big mistake, more often than not, we place the warm, soft neck of sexual intimacy on the cold slab of the sacrificial altar.

The time has come to be completely honest with yourself. You probably know this on a subconscious level, and it's likely why this guide piqued your interest. You know something needs to change—no, to *improve.* Something needs to give, and if you don't address this issue now...then *when?*

Read through the following statements. Reflect on each and answer truthfully, yes or no.

- ✓ The intimate connection with your partner has steadily weakened over time.
- ✓ The passion and desire vanished somewhere along the way.
- ✓ Your sex life has become boring, predictable, lifeless, or non-existent.
- ✓ Communication has deteriorated to the point where it seems, well, *pointless.*
- ✓ You have the desire to renew the bond of sexual intimacy with your partner.
- ✓ You are willing to improve sexual intimacy but unsure how to begin the process.

- ✓ You are both still invested in your relationship.
- ✓ You long to feel sexual desire for your partner again.
- ✓ Your mind is open to receive this relationship-changing information provided in this guide.

Regardless of your answers, kudos for being honest with yourself and acknowledging where your relationship is today. Use this personal feedback as a valuable reference point as you move through the ten keys in this guide.

Responsibility and the Remedy

This guide is about bringing awareness to the importance of sexual intimacy and how to revitalize this core component in your relationship. It's about reconnecting and embracing your sexuality on a deeper level. It's about learning to reopen communication with your partner. To achieve these goals, you must take the appropriate steps to improve sexual intimacy from your side. That said, the first step in this journey begins with Y-O-U.

Of course, your partner is also responsible for the condition of your relationship. I have a good idea of some important elements he has stopped bringing to the table, so believe me, he doesn't get a free pass. However, it's time to be honest with yourself and take responsibility for choices you've made, *or have neglected to make,* for your relationship to be where it is today.

To concede that relationship issues are a result of your actions is a relatively difficult step to take. I understand completely. It is inherently easier to put your guard up, be defensive, and place the blame externally. Nevertheless, it is crucial to take ownership of your part if you sincerely want to improve the status quo. Take a deep breath, drop your guard, open your mind, and be willing to look at the whole picture...beginning with yourself.

Would you agree that rekindling a fire is a fairly involved task? You can't just strike a match and *poof!* Fire! No, you must poke it, stoke it, rearrange it, blow into it...you've got to work it! Only then can you see embers turn to flame. The fire in your sexual relationship did not extinguish overnight, and it will not become an inferno overnight either. Remember this analogy and be patient as you move through this guide. Rebuilding sexual intimacy is a process so it *will* take time. It will. But your hard work, dedication, and consistency will undoubtedly be worth your time and effort. It *will* pay off for both of you because revitalizing this aspect ultimately strengthens the whole relationship. The best part is this—

you and your partner have complete control over this amazing transformation!

Communicate to your partner you are exploring ways to make positive changes in your relationship. By default, he will be a participant, and you want him to be onboard. Unless he has truly left the building, I feel confident he will be thrilled that you're reading a guide about *Sexual Intimacy Matters*. I hope he will be an active and willing participant throughout this process of growth.

Through sexual exploration of possibly some uncharted territory, you will work, I mean *actively work*, on rebuilding a stronger and healthier physical and emotional connection with your partner. At the end of each chapter, you will work on three actionable steps towards making improvements. Intended for introspection, **Honest Assessments** are questions that provide an opportunity for reflection and to objectively assess certain aspects of your relationship. Next, you will find one or more **Sexercise Activities** to execute. Sexercises are action-based challenges to apply your newly acquired knowledge. You will also have a chance to collect your thoughts and record Sexercise experiences through journaling. If you choose to purchase the companion journal, **My SIM Journal**, it follows along with this guide. Journaling offers the possibility for honest self-reflection during this important journey of sexual and emotional exploration. I highly encourage you to fearlessly journal your innermost feelings. Finally, at the end of the guide, you will find a year of **Continuing Sexercises** plus a lengthy list of **Sexual Intimacy Ideas.**

There are few things in life as rewarding as learning something new and then applying your newfound knowledge. This is called transformation. *Sexual Intimacy Matters* is an authentic learning and growing experience that leads to step-by-step, positive transformation.

Without a doubt, it takes a serious, honest, and meaningful effort to reestablish the bond of sexual intimacy. However, by taking a lighthearted and adventurous approach, you and your partner will remember exactly why you fell in love in the first place. I sincerely hope you find a renewed sense of love, appreciation, and desire for one another throughout this journey.

To begin, start by filling out the first page of your journal to set your intention(s). Think about these statements and answer them honestly. It's very helpful to stay on course if you clearly understand your objective. Reflect and complete the following statements.

My SIM Journal

I began this journey on

____

I feel compelled to explore this guide about sexual intimacy matters because

____

____

____

Our current sex life is

____

____

____

Our bond of sexual intimacy is

____

____

____

I believe our sex life is where it is today because

____

____

____

I feel I am responsible for our lack of sexual intimacy because

I feel he is responsible for our lack of sexual intimacy because

By investing my time and effort in this area of my relationship, the goal(s) I hope to achieve is/are

The most important change(s) I would like to see happen is/are

The Relationship Zones

Once upon a time.... *Ah, yes.* The fairy tale. You and your partner were crazy about each other when you first met. Madly in love and brimming with lust. You couldn't eat, sleep, or breathe without thinking about each other. This was it! He was the man of your dreams. It was magical, wasn't it? The deep connection you shared, the excitement you felt when apart, and how you could not get enough of each other when you were together. You were in your own little world, and it just felt *so right,* didn't it? In fact, this man was so incredible, you decided to spend the rest of your life with him.

Let's not forget about how sex is undeniably the best when you're in love. It's as though you're magnetized to each other, and every sensation is ultra-heightened. Do you remember? You couldn't keep your hands off each other for more than five minutes, and you'd feel a tingle in your panties by just looking at him. There was endless affection, whispering sweet nothings to each other, and hot, passionate sex every day, sometimes multiple times a day! I bet you thought your strong desire for him would never fade, right? Say nothing about the fact that one day you would find yourself reaching for the lube to help get things going down there!

So, what do you suppose happened? I believe long-term relationships naturally progress through different zones. According to Dr. Me, there are three main zones in a long-term relationship: the Bliss Zone, the Comfort Zone, and the Danger Zone. Let's break them down, shall we?

The Bliss Zone

The Bliss Zone is what I just described. The beginning of the relationship is amazing, exciting, carefree, and filled with such sweetness and love pouring endlessly from both of you. It's almost nauseating for others to watch. Nothing matters except for spending every moment together and enjoying each other on every level. Falling in love is one of the most wonderful experiences life has to offer, isn't it? There's nothing like it, and I hope every woman has the chance to experience this amazing time at least once in her life.

The Bliss Zone is such an incredible time, and riding the natural high of love feels *so good.* One special desire accompanies these overwhelming feelings of love: to please him. Do you remember your efforts to keep him enamored? You probably bought new clothes and shoes. You bought plenty of sexy underwear and lingerie. You always shaved your legs silky smooth. You invested time and care into your hair and makeup, and you visited the nail salon religiously for manicures and pedicures. You laughed at all his jokes, funny or not. You were over-the-top sweet, oozed sexiness, happily stroked his ego with flirtatious behavior, showered him with affection galore, and simply adored him in every imaginable way.

Fast forward...

The Comfort Zone

You made the mutual decision to take your relationship to the next level and spend your lives together. You made it official by getting married or moving in together and oh, what an amazing and wonderful part of the journey!

This stage of your relationship was new and fresh but in a different way. It was more solid, more real and less fairytale, but incredible just the same. Once you moved past the excitement of life's monumental events of getting married or moving in together, buying a house, establishing careers, and starting a family, you settled into your new life. After all, your relationship couldn't sustain the Bliss Zone forever, and so your relationship naturally progressed into the Comfort Zone.

You're now beyond comfortable with each other. So comfortable in fact, your morning alarm is when he stirs from his slumber and farts. ***Loud.*** And finally, *finally*, he gets the privilege of seeing you without makeup and, dare I say, leg stubble.

Life is still good, right?

Yes, it is. However, as time marches forward, you wonder how on earth these exciting milestones in your life have also become some of the biggest stressors. You're extremely busy balancing your career and/or your little ones, on top of cooking, cleaning, grocery shopping, and on and on. The responsibilities women assume are endless and juggling all these responsibilities can feel overwhelming. Have you found that being so busy with your new life has affected your libido? If so, this is not uncommon by any stretch of the imagination.

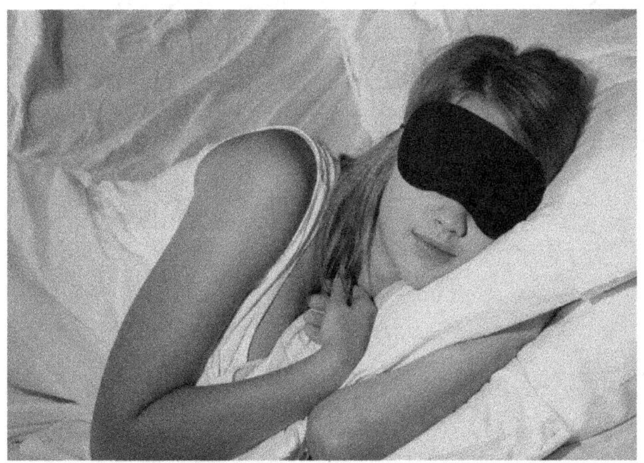

All you want to do at the end of a long day is tuck the kiddos into bed without drama (good luck with that one), take a nice hot shower, put on your comfy jammies, and pray to the god of slumber your children will offer the courtesy of an uninterrupted night sleep *for once.* You crawl into bed and somehow, it feels extra comfortable, probably because you're utterly exhausted. You turn off your nightstand light, pull your eye mask down from your forehead, nestle your body in your favorite sleeping position, and give your bestie a big squeeze. (This would be your pillow, of course!)

Ahhhh...here it comes...beautiful rest. You're so relieved the day is done.

And just as you begin to fade into the dream world, in comes your man, hopping onto the bed all bright-eyed and bushy-tailed. After all, you got into bed only seven minutes before him, so he innocently thought you were still awake. But he was wrong. He startles you from near-sleep and causes your heart to pound in your chest like a jackhammer.

He leans over and whispers, "Hey honey...*pssst*...are you still awake?" You're completely annoyed because he just derailed your train to Dreamland. You make a long and exaggerated sigh as you turn your head and lift one corner of your eye mask. He pays no attention to the icy daggers you shoot through your exposed evil eye as he proceeds to repeatedly tap your ass cheek with his hard-on, like he's knocking on a door. And you say, "*Excuse me,* what do you think *you're* doing? You want to have sex *now?* [Audible scoff.] It's too late." You think to yourself, *Yeah right, like that's going to happen.*

You tell yourself, "Maybe tomorrow night," so you don't feel neglectful. Even though you're still slightly perturbed he startled you, you let him down gently and explain how exhausted you are (which is true) and promise him morning sex before the kids get up (which is untrue). You hope to get a little sympathy from him, but ultimately, you know you just rejected him *again* and bruised his ego *again.* Minor feelings of guilt swim in your head as you kiss him goodnight and tell him you love him. Your inner voice chimes in with its two cents to remind you to make more of an effort to satisfy your man. And you want to. You do. But even though you may feel mentally willing, your body does not feel physically able. *Damn, doesn't he get tired too?* you think to yourself as you readjust your eye mask, settle back into your sleeping position, and drift into a heavenly sleep.

It's unbelievably common for many long-term relationship couples to experience the progression of the sexual downslide. It's not an intentional or calculated act, but life happens. If you're not paying attention, your once intense physical connection can weaken. If you let the sexual aspect of your relationship take its natural downward course, your sex life can become a mundane routine, a rare occurrence, or even worse, non-existent.

Overall, your relationship shifts and evolves through the Comfort Zone. Let's be honest...I mean, it's just you and me here. Sex can be one of the easiest things to remove from your busy daily schedule. With cunning persuasion, your inner voice can effortlessly convince you that it's just *one more thing* to add to your to-do list.

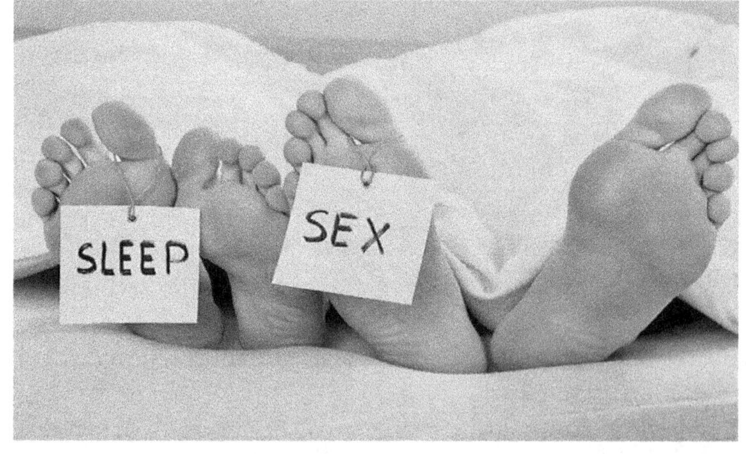

This mental shift can become a real challenge for your partner who likely has a totally different mindset. Though he fights through his own crazy and busy day, somehow, someway, he miraculously still has the energy and desire to have sex just as often as you did during the Bliss Zone.

If an imbalance occurs and this issue remains unaddressed, it could potentially manifest into undesirable situations and create a host of unnecessary problems. This would be the Danger Zone, a place you want to avoid at all cost.

Honest Assessment

1. Assuming your relationship is in the Comfort Zone, how long would you say it's been there?

2. Does it seem like the interest to be sexually active is lop-sided? If so, who is more interested?

3. Approximately how often do you have sex in a week, month, or year?

4. Do you reject his sexual advances? If so, how many times would you estimate you reject him in a week or month?

YES / SOMETIMES / NO

5. If you are the pursuer, does he ever reject your advances?

YES / SOMETIMES / NO

6. Is your weakened desire related to him directly, or is it the indirect result of other reasons (i.e., too busy, too tired, kids, work, etc.)?

7. How is your overall experience of sex? Do you still enjoy it on any level? Do you feel repulsed? Or do you only go through the physical motions because sex has become like a duty?

Sexercise: Create A List

Find time to sit down together for about ten minutes. Open your phone's notepad app and enter the following information in your respective phones:

- List three to five non-sexual activities you enjoyed at the beginning of your relationship.
- List three to five sexual activities you enjoyed at the beginning of your relationship.
- List three to five personality and/or physical traits that attracted you to your partner at the beginning of your relationship.

Reconvene with your completed lists within a day. When you come back together, discuss your responses. Did you list any of the same activities? Take note. Were there any sexual activities that were the same? Again, take note. Of all the activities both sexual and non-sexual, discuss whether you miss any of them. Are either of you interested in reintroducing any of these activities?

After your conversation, exchange your lists so you can reference each other's answers. Narrow down one couple activity and one sexual activity you both noted. Make a date to enjoy these activities, just like way back when. It's possible this Sexercise might just be the spark that relights your fire!

There will be another Honest Assessment and Sexercise in the Danger Zone section of this chapter. Split the time between the two Sexercises how you see fit but try to accomplish them both within a two-week time frame.

My SIM Journal

Write in your journal which relationship elements you feel are lacking. Perhaps it is affection, sexual intimacy, communication, excitement, passion, friendship, bonding, or fun activities. If all these elements are missing, or others, write them down. Take a few moments to think about why these aspects of your relationship have faded, then write at least one possible solution for each element.

* * *

Acknowledgment is key. Once you've acknowledged what's missing, set your intention to step up your efforts to reestablish these missing elements and to incorporate them back into your relationship in a meaningful and sustainable way.

The Danger Zone

Do you feel there may be unspoken contention festering between you and your partner, perhaps involving a lack of sexual intimacy? If so, this may be due to a steady decline in sexual activity. However, other issues in the relationship can crop up and remain unresolved as well. These unaddressed conflicts often create an undercurrent of dissatisfaction in your relationship.

Unfortunately, if no one identifies and attempts to remedy these problems, your relationship can wind up in the Danger Zone.

The Danger Zone is an unsettling stage in your relationship. You and your partner have reached complete frustration with each other concerning intimacy issues, compounded by a multitude of other miscommunications and misunderstandings. Because you have not resolved individual issues as they have occurred through open communication and compromise, a buildup of resentment and blame has developed, causing a foggy haze of dissension that hangs in the air.

The following scenario is a typical Danger Zone argument. It's just one of the many types of conflicts that can occur if your relationship lands in this breeding ground of stubbornness, blame, and overall discontent. This couple has been together for 12 years, and they have three children under nine years of age. Sarah is a stay-at-home mom and Michael is a lawyer.

(The names in this scenario and others have been changed for privacy.)

***

Sarah: *Seriously?* It's almost 9 pm and you're just getting home from work *now,* Michael? *WOOOW!* Great timing now that I've done EVERYTHING myself! Since 3 o'clock this afternoon, I've picked up the kids from school, cooked dinner for them, cleaned the kitchen, took them to their sports practices ALONE, got them cleaned and ready for bed, read them each a story and tucked them into bed...BY MYSELF! I am *so sick* of you making excuses! Because you're so caught up in your work, you leave me alone with these kids all the time, even at night!

I need a break once in a while, and you're *never* here! *What?* I only deserve a break when I close my eyes at night to sleep? You're not even a part of this family anymore! I feel like I'm a single mother doing everything on my own! What is it? Do you stay at work on purpose, so you don't have to bother fulfilling your roles as husband and father? I am *so tired* of making excuses for you to your children why their father is never here. What exactly *is* the point of you being here, anyway? YOU ARE NEVER HERE, you neglectful and inconsiderate bastard! You have a wife and kids who mean *nothing* to you! Way to go...I'm sure you'll win husband and father of the year award!

Michael: *Really?* Is that what you think? I'm out WORKING late because I am the PROVIDER for this family! I *have* to work to take care of MY responsibilities, but *you* don't want to see that little detail! All you want to do is find any fault with me and pick me apart until you've completely emasculated me. YES! I am working a lot because I *have* to! Who else is going to pay all these bills around here?

But that works just fine for me because I'm invisible to you, anyway! I don't even exist to you

anymore except as a paycheck! All you do is bitch and complain about everything! You don't touch me anymore or even look at me, and you stopped having sex with me a long time ago! Why do you want me here? So you can treat me like I'm one of the kids? So I can be your verbal punching bag? Or better yet, so you can ignore me the way you always do? You even treat the dog better than you treat me! I get NO respect around here, no attention, and definitely no appreciation! At least when I'm at work, I get those things from my colleagues and staff! You've even turned my own kids against me! You just take me for granted and treat me like I'm insignificant, and I am SICK OF IT!

* * *

What Sarah and Michael are trying to say to each other has become so convoluted because of their sheer buildup of frustration with each other. The conversation, if you can even call it that, has evolved into a warped version of their true feelings. They simply cannot communicate constructively because they are both at their wit's end and therefore, far beyond the point of healthy communication. Anger has corrupted understandable, heartfelt emotions, which has polluted the tone of their dialogue with one another. Let's erase the overtones of frustration, so we can read between the lines of this argument.

Sarah's true feelings: When you're gone for so long every day, I feel lonely, and I feel like I don't have a partner, either for myself or to help raise our children. You are my husband and the father of our children. That is very special to me *and* to them. We love you, and we miss you. We don't like when you're not around. I feel like your job has become more important to you than your family. I feel like our children are missing out on wonderful childhood experiences and memories with their father, and I hate that for them. I'm so alone, and I don't know how to express to you anymore how horrible that feels.

Yes, I've lost the desire to have sex with you because it would almost feel as though I was lying with a stranger. We have grown so far apart as a couple, and it's only getting worse. I am beyond frustrated, and I really don't know how to move forward.

Michael's true feelings: I work so much, not because I want to, but because I have to. It is my responsibility to provide for this family, and the only way to do that is to work hard so I can give you and the kids a comfortable lifestyle. I *do* miss you and the kids. I *do* want to be a part of their lives and yours. But the truth is, I feel completely invisible to you since we've had kids. I miss the way you would come up and hug me from behind all the time, and the way you would be playful and act all sexy towards me and make an effort to excite me. It really bothers me you don't even touch me or have any sexual desire for me anymore. I feel like I'm no longer a man in your eyes, but just another one of your kids. I feel unappreciated for what I'm trying to do for this family and that really hurts me. Our bond has clearly broken, and I don't even know if it can be fixed.

I'm so frustrated by all this, so when there's an opportunity to stay longer at work, I do, because I am at a loss of how to fix all these problems that don't seem to have a beginning or an end. I hide behind my work because I feel totally helpless about what to do with our situation.

Sarah and Michael don't know how to remedy the problem because it's not just one problem anymore. Over time, they have slowly gotten buried under a myriad of problems in their relationship.

* * *

A healthy dialogue between two people requires not only calm reflection and emotional intelligence, but brutal self-honesty and courage from both sides. That's a very tall order for anyone. When a relationship lands in the Danger Zone, it can feel downright hopeless that you will ever communicate amicably again, much less see eye to eye. If your relationship has landed in this unstable and stress-filled zone, take some time for honest reflection about why you believe things got to this point. Begin to break down communication barriers by taking the following actions.

Take responsibility for your contribution to the problems. Stay far, far away from pointing your finger at your partner for all the problems in your relationship. Doing so only keeps you in the vicious cycle of the blame-game because he will more than likely respond by pointing his finger right back at you.

Remember, one of the most crucial parts of this journey is to learn how to self-examine your actions, non-actions, and interactions with your partner so you can make positive changes from your side.

Be empathetic and genuinely try to understand his perspective. It isn't easy to put the shoe on the other foot. In fact, it's quite difficult because it requires removing yourself from feelings of anger or righteousness. However, if you can get yourself into the habit of viewing situations from an empathetic point of view, it can be an eye-opening experience. Learn to see situations from his vantage point and ask if he would be willing to see situations from yours. You can gain great insight into each other's feelings through the practice of empathy.

Really listen to what your partner is saying. While in a state of anger or stubbornness, what is **said** and what is **meant** are typically not in alignment. Read between the lines of what he is trying to convey, like in the second example above. Focus on keywords your partner expresses and stop for a moment to examine the validity of his words. Do they hold any truth? Introspection can be challenging because it forces us to look at ourselves in a raw way, and it can be painful to learn things about ourselves that are unappealing.

If you recognize your relationship is in fact in the Danger Zone and you do nothing to remedy this, things can progressively slide further down a precarious slope towards even *bigger* issues. And oh, how you will want to avoid those messy, tangled webs created by unresolved communication problems!

Honest Assessment

1. Has your relationship ever been in the Danger Zone?

YES / NO

2. If so, are you still there or did you work through your issues?

---

3. How do you feel your relationship got to this place?

---

4. Can you pinpoint when your communication began to break down?

---

5. In what ways did poor communication create resentment?

---

6. Do you feel frustrated because you continue to hit the same wall or spin in the same old cycles?

YES / NO

7. If you are in this difficult place, do you feel a sense of hopelessness or hopefulness about your relationship?

Sexercise

What do you feel is the biggest point of contention between you and your partner? Is it mutual, such as financial troubles? Is it the change of going from "just the two of us" to juggling the demands of a family? Or are the little, everyday stressors creating a wedge to the point where you both have minimal tolerance for everything...*including* each other?

Have A Heartfelt Conversation

Does this seem simple? Well, it's not even close. To come to your partner with your heart in your hand and your defenses down is, let's face it, much easier said than done. If animosity has festered over time, it might feel uncomfortable approaching these difficult topics with the sensitivity required to make positive and sustainable changes. But go ahead...open up with pure honesty and a sense of surrender because you don't want to fight anymore, do you?

Tell him your true feelings about the parts of your relationship you feel have deteriorated. This conversation is not about accusation; rather, it's about acknowledgment. Explain to him what makes you upset and why. Express what makes you feel disappointed or what makes you feel sadness. If you approach your partner in a non-defensive way with the intention to heal and not fight, there's a high probability you will get the same constructive communication from him, which should be reciprocated with the same level of understanding from you.

Agree that you're both going to find at least three actionable ways to work on making positive changes as a result of this heartfelt conversation. Get back together within two or three days to discuss the action steps you're going to take in order to make these positive changes happen.

My SIM Journal

After your conversation, write in your journal about how it felt to share your feelings. What was his reaction? Was he defensive, receptive, or understanding? Reflect on your conversation and write down what he expressed to you. Listening from a place of openness, were you able to understand his concerns or dissatisfaction? Do you feel there's a likelihood for positive change after this conversation?

* * *

It may not feel like it, but you're making excellent strides in your communication efforts. Pat yourself on the back! This isn't easy stuff, but I'm very proud of you for opening your heart and taking these potentially uncomfortable steps.

Most relationships experience the Bliss and Comfort Zones. Ultimately, you want to avoid the Danger Zone. If your relationship has settled in this zone and you have a strong desire to turn things around, you must both acknowledge where it's at, how things got here, and what you will do to make improvements. If you both commit to work hard on communication and handling situations with greater awareness and empathy, you will steadily climb out of the Danger Zone.

Listen, no matter what the current condition of your relationship is, it should *not* feel like a death sentence, or that you're doomed to spend the rest of your life unhappy. Being in a long-term relationship means you have a partner for life, so feel blessed by this gift. Because it *is* a gift. There are so many single people out there, lonely, desperate, and wishing to share their lives with a partner. You are so lucky you found someone you connected with enough to want to spend your life with them. Try to appreciate this gift once again if you have lost sight of it and work hard through this guide to recover the happiness and enjoyment you once felt.

KEY ONE
Unspoken Communication

Whew. Sarah and Michael had reached a complete deadlock in their communication, wouldn't you agree? What started as subtle changes in their relationship eventually created a full communication breakdown. It was like a two-way radio with an increasingly warped signal. Both shouted all day into the receiver, while the other heard only static. Unfortunately, neither of them could get through to the other.

As we know, communication occurs in many other ways than verbal language. However, we mostly depend on words to express or validate our feelings. In a way, we feel dependent on words to externalize what is inside us. That's natural, and it's the reason we're drawn toward writers or musical artists who can express what we've never been able to put into words. They solve a mystery and complete a work of self-expression for us.

Consider, however, the consequences of relying on words alone. We remain illiterate, or at least not literate enough, even when we are presented with solid information through non-verbal forms of communication. Because of our strong dependence on words, our ability to read between the lines becomes skewed, which can easily cause misinterpretations. We must rectify this great danger if we hope for the healthiest relationship possible.

It is crucial to learn how to navigate these wordless spaces because an enormous amount of information resides in them. Let's take a closer look at the following forms of unspoken communication: listening, silence, actions, and body language. While you're reading through these different communication styles, reflect how each one plays out in your relationship.

Listen

People want to be heard when they feel moved to speak about something. It reassures them that their words have value. When your partner attempts to communicate his wants and needs, even if they may seem trivial or insignificant, how do you respond? Do you dismiss him? Pay vague attention? Ignore him? Get defensive? Become agitated? Do you hear what he's saying to you? Do you *listen?* Do you pay close attention and use body language to convey your interest in his words?

If he attempts to communicate about issues in your relationship, be sensitive about what he's expressing. Validate his concerns by giving him your complete attention. STOP what you're doing, silence and stash your phone, sit down together, look him in the eyes, and focus on his communication. Tune in not only to what he's saying, but also to *how* he's saying it. Listen intently if your partner opens up about anything honestly and humbly. Take the extra step and put yourself in his shoes. It's a great opportunity to exercise your empathy muscle.

If he tries to talk but you see the timing won't permit your full focus, nicely explain that you would rather postpone the conversation until you can give your undivided attention. Your partner may feel vulnerable about sharing his feelings because he doesn't want to be perceived as weak (by you or himself), take the chance of having his feelings dismissed, or run the risk of triggering an argument. These fears can make any man feel hesitant to open up about feelings or concerns. If he displays the slightest vulnerability but opens up anyway, don't shut him down. Let him know you genuinely care so he feels comfortable speaking. Men are not as open as women when it comes to conversing about relationship issues. We naturally want to talk, talk, and talk some more about our problems with our partner, family, friends, and most of all, our hairdresser!

Unfortunately, some men completely avoid these types of conversations, so there's not even a chance for an unhealthy situation to improve. If your man shares his feelings, be wise, listen sincerely, and take his words to heart. Treat him how you want to be treated. Bring understanding, compassion, and the comfort of a good friend to the table. Make him feel secure about confiding his desires or discontent regarding certain aspects of your relationship. Try not to become defensive, emasculate him, or make him feel like his needs are insignificant. These types of responses are counterproductive and will only invalidate his feelings. I think we can all agree that it feels terrible when someone close to us dismisses our emotions.

It's also very important to show you're listening with your whole body. Use posture, nodding, and facial expressions to show that you value his bold act. But the buck doesn't stop there. Immediate and sustainable action should take place in response to his concerns or needs. While the act of listening occurs in the moment, the proof of whether a person has been heard happens *afterwards.*

Silence

We like it when people spell things out for us verbally, don't we? It assures us that we understand a situation entirely. However, verbal communication only comprises a fraction of how we interact. There is a plethora of information in the spaces between words. We simply need to tune in to what these silent messages tell us.

Let me share an example. A friend of mine, Ashley, was head-over-heels for this guy, Jason. Because she was so enamored, she was blind to the superficiality of the relationship, which was mostly sexting, which led to, you guessed it...sex. In the beginning, he would text *love you* occasionally, but eventually he stopped. I believe at first, he did have a level of interest more than just sexual get-togethers, but he quickly realized she wasn't his type. She would still text *I love you* and even say it in person, but he no longer responded with words, written or verbal. Why do you suppose he stopped? Did the cat get his tongue? Maybe he broke his texting thumbs? Or, the most likely option, he no longer felt love for her. Even though his *silence* made his lack of love crystal clear, she remained hopelessly confused. In this situation, his silence *was* the communication. Ashley did not want to believe the message so she remained in a prolonged, self-induced state of confusion and denial.

Sometimes we desperately want to hear something vocalized because we hold a *false belief* that words validate the truth. Anyone can say anything they want, but that doesn't mean those words are valid. What if Jason kept telling Ashley he loved her out of guilt? His words would have been a complete lie, filled with emptiness. She refused to believe his message of silence because she didn't want to accept reality. But if she had paid attention to his absence of words, she could have saved herself a lot of time and avoidable pain.

Can you think of any issues in your relationship where your words are met with silence? Alternatively, do you use silence to communicate certain feelings? Raise your awareness about what his silence tells you and what your silence conveys to him.

Actions

We all know the old cliché, *actions speak louder than words*. Do you overlook this glaring form of communication, or do you mindfully observe other people's actions? How about in your relationship? Do your partner's words sync with his actions? If he says he loves you, do his actions support that? If he says he's still attracted to you, is he flirtatious and does he compliment you? If he says he wants to make you happy, does he do anything to make you happy?

On the flip side, take a self-examination to make sure your words and actions align with your feelings. If you're still attracted to him, do you show him affection or pursue him to be sexually intimate? Do caring gestures accompany your professions of love? Actions tell the real story of your feelings. Check yourself to ensure your actions and words align. If not, make necessary adjustments. If his actions and words are mismatched, gently share your observations. I believe the alignment of our words and actions says an awful lot about our integrity. Would you agree?

Body Language

We're all well versed in this form of unspoken language. According to statistics, we use body language to communicate the most with others. Consider how possible it is to have a conversation, even with strangers, using only facial expressions, posture, and gestures. Or you can have a detailed conversation with a girlfriend through eye movements alone. You can even tell your child they've done something wrong simply by the way you stand in their bedroom doorway without ever opening your mouth.

If you're angry when your man comes home late again, how do you greet him? With a warm smile and a sweet hello? Um, I doubt it. You probably meet him with a raised eyebrow, a stern look at your cell phone for the time, and possibly even some hand-on-hip action. How about when he's going through a rough time? You probably hug him lovingly, rub his back gently, and give him a reassuring look that everything will be okay.

Does your body language ever send a sexual message? When he comes home from work, have you ever waited in bed for him? Or when you walk by him, do you ever grab him or give him a sexy and flirtatious look to indicate you're interested in being intimate? When he climbs into bed, he might start rubbing your thigh, kiss your shoulder, or place your hand between his legs. You then respond through body language. If you're interested, you engage in his advances. If not, you push his hand away, grumble a few words, and turn over, showing complete disinterest.

These examples show how much we communicate non-verbally. Become mindful of the messages your body language sends and see if there's a pattern, positive or negative. Also observe what his body language tells you. There is a ton of information he's sharing. *What is it?* Train yourself to become a keen observer of subtle body language. This style of communication alone can offer a tremendous amount of information about your relationship.

If ALL your communication skills don't become tack-sharp and you allow communication to slip away, the day will inevitably come (if it hasn't already) when you ask yourself, *What happened to our strong connection? Who is this stranger? Why don't I feel anything anymore? When on earth did this happen? Jeez, we don't even talk except about work or the kids.* To avoid these thoughts, you must keep a constant dialog about everything significant *and* insignificant in your lives. Talk about sex, love, intimacy, goals, emotions, hardships, dreams, feelings, finances, child-rearing, fears, concerns, desires, work-related topics...share everything!

Heighten your awareness about different communication styles and how you can improve upon them. Communicate non-verbally by genuinely **listening.** Pay attention to **silence** and its messages. Observe **actions** and notice if they align with the words spoken. Become more aware of what your **body language** tells each other. Take the first step and encourage him to follow your lead. Being on the same page leads to a more caring, open, and communicative relationship. Understanding the importance of all forms of communication is a necessary component for moving through the Ten Essential Keys.

Honest Assessment

1. Are you in tune with the languages of unspoken communication in your relationship?

YES / SOMETIMES / NO

2. Take a few minutes to think about how these four different communication styles play out between you and your partner. Are they mostly positive, negative, or a mix?

____

____

____

3. Rate your overall communication, both spoken and unspoken, in your relationship from 1 (in the pits) to 10 (awesome).

____

____

____

4. If you rank below a five, can you pinpoint when your communication started to slip? After kids? After a big promotion at work? After your in-laws moved in down the street? Oh, I'm just kidding...that would be bliss, *right?*

____

____

____

5. Do you pay attention and *listen* to your partner when he's speaking about a serious topic? How about a casual conversation?

YES / SOMETIMES / NO

6. Do you follow through on his requests/needs after he's expressed them?

YES / SOMETIMES / NO

7. Do you use silence to communicate, or even as a consequence, when you get upset with your partner?

YES / SOMETIMES / NO

8. Are your words authenticated by your actions?

YES / SOMETIMES / NO

9. What are the three most common body language signals you send to your partner? Is there a pattern? For example, is it mostly impatience/frustration or flirtation/playfulness?

____

____

____

Sexercise: Raise Your Awareness

Of all the ways we communicate non-verbally, body language is used the most to communicate with others, though we use it subconsciously. To RAISE YOUR AWARENESS, conduct a 5-day observation about just how much you and your partner's body language reveals about your relationship. Since you will be recording this observation, stay mindful not to overlook or distort in your mind your natural, baseline behaviors. Self-examination can be tricky, but authentic reflection is a must for growth and positive change.

Record in your journal everything you notice about your body language exchanges during this Sexercise. To get you started on the right track, here are some examples of common body language signals.

When either of you arrive home from work, is there any physical interaction such as a kiss or hug? Or do you barely acknowledge each other? If he tells you about something that happened at work, do you sit down and engage, ask questions, and show a genuine interest in his story? Or do you continue to go about whatever you're doing, barely look in his direction, and offer only one-word responses? If you ask him to go to the farmer's market on a Saturday morning, does he willfully agree and happily peruse the market with you right by your side? Or does he go, but pouts and gives you an attitude like you're dragging your 5-year-old son to go shoe shopping with you, completely killing your joy of the moment?

Take any opportunity you can to practice body language awareness. This Sexercise will force you to see your true feelings about each other, teach you to become less reliant on words, and help you to focus on the facts. I believe you will gain tremendous insight after your 5-day observation.

My SIM Journal

After writing your observations from this Sexercise, reread and reflect on the information you gathered. Was your non-verbal language more towards the positive or negative side? Passive or aggressive? Engaged or distant? Then write in your journal what you feel each of the unspoken languages revealed about your relationship. Take a close look at these forms of communication from a purely observational perspective and consider if there are ways, starting today, that you could begin to make improvements. If so, write them down.

The Key to Unspoken Communication

The key to unspoken communication is mindfully observing all forms of non-verbal communication. Once you become more aware of just how much information comes from unspoken communication, the door opens to understanding the true condition of **all** your relationships.

KEY TWO
Sexual Communication

Who knew there were so many ways to communicate? Well, we know they exist because we all use them. But are we truly aware of how we apply or *neglect to apply* them in our daily lives? I mean, who thinks about that stuff? But now that we have delved into different communication styles, are you beginning to see their significance?

There is another form of communication so imperative to a healthy relationship that it deserves a chapter of its own. I'm talking about **sexual communication.** This form can get so easily lost in translation. Why? Because it's a delicate topic. It's intimate. It's personal. It can even evoke embarrassment, guilt, and shame. It can be a difficult subject to broach because it can feel awkward, raw, or uncomfortable.

Although you may want to run away from the subject, **intentional conversations about your sex life are monumentally important to improve and maintain communication in this department.** When you open this dialog, you create an opportunity to bring this part of your relationship back to life and to make it feel fresh and exciting again.

As noted earlier, sex can become mundane, boring, and predictable outside the Bliss Zone. When a couple drifts apart sexually, it can create problems in other areas of their relationship. I'm sure we'd all like to steer clear of unnecessary problems, right? I mean, I sure don't need them—the stress of everyday life is more than enough! Let's take a look at two examples of sexual communication, one unhealthy and one healthy, to understand why the latter is much better for your overall relationship.

Unhealthy vs Healthy Sexual Communication

Unhealthy

Here's just one example of unhealthy sexual communication. The following scenario frames how the horrible cycle of the blame-game can tail-spin a relationship out of control.

* * *

Elizabeth and Dillon went through the natural decline of physical interaction during their eight-year marriage. Although they had a seemingly good relationship, it was filled with many responsibilities along with the stressors of everyday life. They were busy raising their two young kids of three and five years of age. They also ran a successful web-design company together out of their home. As time passed, they only got together sexually about once or twice a month. During the stretches of time without sex, Dillon didn't satisfy himself, so he had no endurance when they finally had sex. It would be over in literally two minutes.

Elizabeth received zero satisfaction from such a quick interaction. For her, it was a race against the clock to have an orgasm, knowing how soon it would end. Most of the time she didn't even bother trying because she knew his staying power was nonexistent, which was very frustrating. When they spoke about this issue, Dillon said his endurance was so low because the wait was too long. Elizabeth was compassionless because she never got satisfied. The conflict was like the long-running unsolved riddle: *Which came first...the chicken or the egg?*

Elizabeth and Dillon held firm on their positions, and it became a huge point of contention between them. They simply could not get past the blame-game. The vicious cycle eventually spiraled out of control, and the high level of animosity created irritations unrelated to the core problem. Their patience grew shorter as business partners and parents. They couldn't figure out how to articulate their frustrations without being accusatory, how to communicate their true feelings, or how to compromise. They were simply stuck in the quicksand of blame, righteousness, and stubbornness.

* * *

Unless both people recognize and rectify issues with effective communication, a problem that starts as a small wedge can turn into a gaping chasm. Elizabeth and Dillon could have avoided this situation if they communicated their true feelings and worked together as a team for a solution, rather than being obstinate and blaming each other.

Have you ever been caught in the blame-game cycle? One little issue can turn into an uncontrolled battle of the wills. When two people dig in their heels so deeply, it becomes a stalemate. Why? Because stubbornness and defiance will never create a win-win scenario.

Healthy

Now, when healthy sexual communication is at play in a long-term relationship, *WOW...* talk about exciting! When a couple maintains an ongoing dialog about wants, needs, issues, desires, and preferences, the bond of sexual intimacy strengthens over time. Couples who work (because it does take work) to keep this bond intact, enjoy an amazing opportunity to experience sexual exploration and satisfaction on a much deeper level. Although it does require a joint effort from both people to keep sexual energy strong and thriving, doing so creates a positive flow throughout the whole relationship, because remember...it's all connected.

Do you want to open the door to improved sexual communication with your partner? To get exactly what you both desire in the bedroom, **the absolute best time to talk about anything sex-related is immediately following sex!** Why? Well, think about it. You're both naked (or close to it), vulnerable, and probably feeling open and relaxed to discuss this topic, which at other times may feel taboo or uncomfortable to speak about.

Although Angel and I speak freely about sexual intimacy anytime because it's a topic we're both very comfortable discussing, we usually talk about sex right after being intimate. We talk about things like the session itself and what we enjoyed the most. We compliment each other, and talk about what we would like to do next time or in the future. We share when our minds aren't completely present and why, the intensity of our orgasms, our desires, if there's a reason for a temporary decline in sexual activity or interest, past sexual interactions with each other, fantasies, etc.

I've also discovered this is a great time to share an idea to try something brand new or tell him what I think would arouse me. He's not a mind-reader. He'll never know if I don't tell him. The same goes for him. If he doesn't share with me what he would enjoy or if he wants to try something new, how will I ever know? I strongly encourage you to use this window of opportunity to speak candidly about all things sex-related.

As you've learned from the first two keys, multiple communication forms are continuously at play between you and your partner. Since communication is such a critically important aspect of a healthy relationship, you must stay acutely aware to keep all lines of communication open and clear.

Is it possible to reach the milestone in your relationship where you're so in sync with each other you'll never experience hardships, challenges, or difficulties again? Eh, probably not. Well actually, no. However, if you remain dedicated to keeping communication lines open, compromise whenever possible, and make necessary adjustments to keep each other happy, your relationship will have the greatest chance of success.

Remember, people are ever evolving, growing, and changing. Because of this, your relationship will always be in a continuous state of readjustment. Stay mindfully aware of this as you move through the years together.

Honest Assessment

1. Do you feel your relationship has healthy sexual communication? Why or why not?

2. Do you feel like your sexual needs are being met? If so, how? If not, what do you feel is missing?

3. Do you feel like your partner's sexual needs are being met? If so, what are you doing to meet them? If not, what do you believe you could do to meet them?

4. When was the last time you had a conversation that revolved solely around your sexual relationship? Was the exchange positive or negative?

5. Do you feel like you're able to communicate your sexual needs? Does he communicate his needs? Are you open or closed-off? How about him?

---

6. How would you rate your overall sex life on a scale from 1 to 10? If it's below a five, what are some ways you feel you can make improvements? If it's five or above, is there still room for improvement or do you feel you're doing everything you can?

---

7. Have you ever engaged in a post-sex conversation? If so, did any positive action happen as a result of your communication?

Sexercise: *Oh, You Know What's Coming!* The Sex Talk

As difficult as this Sexercise may seem, it's a necessary point of growth that will help open your relationship to a new world of sexual intimacy. As you move deeper into this guide, you will understand the necessity of this step. The initial conversation may feel a little uncomfortable, but hey, you got this! I know you do! After the first talk, it becomes easier and easier. In fact, you will both look forward to these post-sex conversations.

This conversation should happen after the next time you have sex. Give yourself enough time afterward, at least 30 minutes to an hour, to engage in this conversation without interruption. Give him the heads-up that you want to speak with him about your sex life. If he's curious, tell him there's no reason to worry.

Cut to...you just finished having sex. Maybe you're both satisfied, maybe not. It doesn't really matter because either way, things are about to get a lot better! Open the conversation with, "Hey, remember I said I wanted to talk about our sex life?" Then go for it! Be clear that you want to have an open and constructive conversation about improving your sex life. Steer clear of arguments, blame, accusations, or guilt-trips. Start by taking responsibility for your contribution to the state of your sex life. Hopefully, he will follow suit. Acknowledge where you feel your sex life is and how you think it landed there. Be empathetic as you listen, and hopefully he will respond with empathy towards you as well.

By the end of the conversation, you both should have taken ownership of where your sexual relationship is today and gained some new insight into each other's perspective. This is awesome because now you can both take actionable steps.

Do not end this conversation without discussing the following topics.

- ✓ Tell each other what you miss the most about your intimate relationship.
- ✓ Acknowledge that you sincerely listened by repeating his key points. Ask him to acknowledge your key points.
- ✓ Discuss some elements you would like to add to your next sex session, and then make a plan for it to happen!

If you continually work on building this important bond, you will naturally feel more relaxed each time you have post-sex conversations. During these talks, be bold and confident while sharing what you would like to do, how you would like to do it, and new things you want to try. Encourage him to do the same.

My SIM Journal

Write in your journal about your first post-sex talk. Were you nervous? Was he engaged? Did he express anything you were unaware of? Did you reach an agreement on how to improve your sexual communication? Did you discuss any new ideas you would like to try or make a commitment to be intimate more often?

Jot down some sexual ideas you want to explore with your partner. Share these ideas the next time you have a post-sex talk. If you need some ideas, check out the *Dare You Challenges* in **Sexual Intimacy Ideas.**

* * *

I hope you understand that you are on the verge of opening a whole new world of fun and excitement through sexual communication! The world of sexuality is vast...explore, explore, explore!

The Key to Sexual Communication

Healthy sexual communication requires constant and open dialog to get exactly what you both desire in the bedroom. Post-sex conversations are the key to keeping your bond of sexual communication strong, exciting, and fresh.

KEY THREE
Confidence!

Disclaimer: Given the complexity and delicate nature of self-confidence, I discuss only the physical aspect of confidence building in this chapter. The following pages include stories of my personal struggles with self-confidence and share with you different ways I've improved it from a physical perspective. As you know, there are a myriad of variables that influence your level of confidence which goes far beyond the physical. This chapter is meant to provide the opportunity for self-reflection, assess where your confidence level is today, and offer some fun and simple ideas to help give it a boost, if you desire to do so.

Let's take a quick recap before we get into this next all-important key to your transformation. You identified which life-scenario(s) led you to read this guide, you learned about the different zones of long-term relationships, and you received a refresher course on several healthy ways to communicate with your partner.

Now it's time to measure your confidence level. If it's low or non-existent, the energy of feeling sexy, sexual, sensual, and desirable will be challenging to tap into. Confidence is by far one of the most essential keys necessary to help you unlock the sexual desire you once possessed effortlessly.

Of course, confidence comes from within, but there *are* outward variables that can shape our self-perception. Maybe someone made hurtful comments when you were young and impressionable, and those painful words have skewed your ability to see your true beauty. Or, maybe you were lucky and had amazing parents who made you feel like the most beautiful and incredible human being on the planet, constantly telling you what a special person you were. From childhood into adulthood, we carry residual feelings connected to our experiences related to self-confidence during our youth. No matter how externally beautiful we may appear to others, those experiences, *especially* negative ones, can echo deeply in our subconscious. It's not really what our eyes see in the mirror...it's what our minds tell us—*that's* what we see.

I have always struggled with confidence, which mostly stems from self-consciousness about a physical flaw I've had my whole life. I was born with a birth defect in my left eye. My retina did not fully develop, leaving me legally blind with a lazy eye. Before the doctor figured out the correct diagnosis, I had to wear an eye patch over my healthy eye for several hours every day. He thought that would strengthen my lazy eye. *Ugh.*

Hindering the ability to see out of the eye I actually *could* see from, I was laughed at by other kids and even adults because I ran into so many objects while I was forced to wear this eye patch. If you think about it, I suppose I just looked like a clumsy, cross-eyed kid playing pirate by myself...they didn't know any better. Perhaps I would've laughed if I saw that too. But the pain of that laughter devastated me. I was too young to articulate to my parents what I experienced emotionally when I wore the eye patch. I felt so humiliated, so embarrassed, and so self-conscious.

By the time I reached the age of eight, the doctor finally figured out I legitimately could *not* see from that eye. Although I had corrective surgery to straighten my eye, to me, it looks glaringly different than my right eye. Forty-plus years later, the wound remains fresh because never have I *ever* once looked in the mirror without noticing the imperfection of my eye. To this very day, I still feel uncomfortable making eye contact with others for too long because I'm self-conscious they will notice.

Although I've tried to develop an amicable relationship with my critical inner voice about this flaw by responding with compassion and self-love, I will not lie and say it's easy. It is hard. Compassion and self-love can be exceptionally difficult for someone who struggles with self-consciousness or low levels of confidence. From my experience, I sincerely understand the battle with confidence and empathize if this has been a struggle for you. I'll share some more stories about my experiences with confidence because I don't want you to feel alone. I also want to offer you encouragement that it is possible to improve this aspect of yourself.

* * *

And so the story goes...

After I had my second son at age 33, my body held on for dear life to the extra weight I could not shed naturally. I was so busy with the responsibilities of a newborn, a toddler, and running a business, when I say I didn't stop to look in the mirror to assess my body after childbirth, believe me, I didn't. About six months after the birth, we visited family and friends in New York who had not seen me since my son was born. Not only one, but a *few* people asked if I was pregnant again. I was shocked!

When we returned home, I immediately made my then-husband John take pictures of me in my bra and underwear from all angles. When I saw those pictures, I lost it! He never said a word about my obvious weight gain. I scolded him for withholding the truth, which was that I appeared to be permanently four months pregnant. His simple reply was this, "I didn't notice because that's not what I see when I look at you."

On one hand, his reply made me melt. He genuinely didn't care and loved me for me, no matter what size I was. On the other hand, I realized I couldn't rely on him to mention any glaring changes in my appearance.

The very next day after my photo shoot I joined a fitness center, and never looked back!

* * *

During that period, I was not in touch with my body or confidence level, whatsoever. How about you? Do you have children? If so, has your body also been through the wringer of childbirth, accompanied by the long, long period afterward when making time for yourself is, well...*laughable?* **Me time** was probably a fact of life when you were single or pre-motherhood, but you honestly can't remember because that seems like another lifetime. If you have indeed lost touch with your appearance and confidence level over the years, I can offer some helpful ideas I've used to level-up my appearance, which translated to a confidence boost. While confidence ultimately comes from within, there *are* ways to increase your confidence level from the outside.

Take this personal assessment to gauge your confidence level. See how much *or little* you're doing for yourself on the exterior to help elevate your confidence level. Checkmark each description that currently applies to you.

Clothing

What's your daily attire?

☐ Dresses—sexy, playful, colorful, any length or style

☐ Tight jeans/stretchy pants, cute shirts that show some cleavage

☐ Spandex workout attire–cool/sexy designs and material

☐ Short shorts, form-fitting shirts that might show a little mid-drift

☐ T-shirts, flannel shirts, jeans/pants

☐ Sweat-suits only

☐ A muumuu 24/7

What do you wear to bed?

☐ Nothing

☐ Sexy underwear

☐ Lingerie

☐ Cotton, silk, or lace nighties

☐ A cami top and underwear

☐ Nightgowns

☐ Sweats and a tee-shirt

☐ Pajama top and bottom

☐ It doesn't matter, just as long as it's clean...or clean*ish*

How would you classify your overall wardrobe?

☐ Flirty

☐ Sexy

☐ Business

☐ Casual

☐ Preppy

☐ Sporty

☐ Classy

- ☐ Elegant
- ☐ Comfortable only
- ☐ You don't give your wardrobe much thought these days

Beauty Regimen

Do you make your fingernails pretty?

- ☐ Weekly at the nail salon
- ☐ Biweekly at the nail salon
- ☐ You do your nails regularly
- ☐ Your nails are natural, never painted

Do you make your toenails pretty?

- ☐ Weekly pedicures at the nail salon
- ☐ Biweekly pedicures at the nail salon
- ☐ Once a month at the nail salon
- ☐ You paint your toenails
- ☐ You leave them natural

Do you wear makeup?

- ☐ Daily, with a re-apply later
- ☐ Daily, once in the morning
- ☐ Randomly throughout the week
- ☐ Weekends only
- ☐ Weekdays only
- ☐ Once a week
- ☐ Natural, you don't own makeup

How about the hair salon? (Highlights, dye, haircuts, hair treatments, blow-outs)

- ☐ Once every 6 to 8 weeks
- ☐ Once every 3 to 6 months

- ☐ Once every 6 to 12 months
- ☐ You go to your Aunt Fannie's basement salon and she trims your ends once in a blue moon...*gratis!*

Do you treat yourself to the spa? (Facials/body massages/body wraps)

- ☐ Once a week
- ☐ Once every two weeks
- ☐ Once a month
- ☐ Once every two months
- ☐ Once every six months
- ☐ Once a year for your birthday or anniversary
- ☐ Never been

Do you have an exercise routine?

- ☐ Daily—it's like breathing to you
- ☐ Every other day
- ☐ Three days a week
- ☐ Once a week
- ☐ Random—only when you can fit it in
- ☐ Exer-*what?* Ha! Never!

What's your beauty rest routine?

- ☐ Wake up naturally with 8 hours minimum of uninterrupted beauty rest (Oh, you lucky dog! Can I live at your house please?)
- ☐ Average 6 to 7 hours with minimal interruptions—maybe just a pee break in the middle of the night
- ☐ Five hours or less because your sleep is constantly being interrupted by crying kids, barking dogs, the cat sitting on your face in the middle of the night, your husband snoring, your neighbor's loud motorcycle at 6 am every...single...morning, or all the above

Grooming

Bush maintenance:

- ☐ Bald eagle
- ☐ Trimmed triangle/landing strip
- ☐ Heart shape
- ☐ Anything goes—depends on your mood
- ☐ All-natural

Body maintenance: (shaving legs, armpits)

- ☐ Daily—you feel like a cactus if you don't shave
- ☐ Every other day
- ☐ Three days a week
- ☐ Once a week is good enough
- ☐ Only when the mood strikes

If you feel the desire to increase your level of confidence from where it's at today, be aware of this more than likely inevitable challenge: feelings of unworthiness and/or guilt. It can be difficult to persuade yourself that you *are* worthy of the monetary and time investment to build outer confidence. This concept is exceptionally challenging if you are a mother. Being the selfless creature you are, it's hard to grant yourself permission to value yourself in this way. I understand this inner struggle all too well. It's so easy to find every reason in the world to put ourselves on the backburner because hey, we're moms and our kids—no... actually, EVERYONE else's needs come before our own. However, it is critical to our overall well-being as women and mothers to move up to the front burner. Okay, maybe it's the smaller front burner, but nevertheless, we need to prioritize ourselves because our energy and mood effects everyone around us. You know the expression, *If mama ain't happy...nobody is.* Whatever you are experiencing internally, good or bad, it's coming out. Wouldn't it be better for everyone, yourself included, to radiate positive vibes?

Rather than feeling guilty about caring for yourself, feel **deserving** of whatever it means to you personally to rebuild confidence, if it needs a bolster. If you are a mother, you make countless sacrifices, **COUNTLESS**. You should **NOT** feel badly about showing yourself the same love and care you show everyone else because if you don't, then honestly, *who the hell will?*

So, my friend, turn off your low-burning backburner, slide forward, and set the flame to high! Remember, confidence building is *not* an act of selfishness; it's an act of genuine self-love. Starting today, set your intention to show yourself at least one daily gesture of love because

YES, you *are* deserving!

This following experience of mine was during a period in my life that I did exactly what I just got done explaining to you. I became hyper-focused on ways to improve my outer appearance and it significantly improved my inner confidence.

* * *

Throughout my late twenties and early thirties, I was a natural, hippie-type chick who was not fond of dressing up or receiving attention. I was a landscape designer in love with nature and all things natural. Dressing up was so far removed from my lifestyle unless it was for a special event, and even then it took a real push to dress up.

I was so busy taking care of my little boys and running our business, my outer appearance was literally the last thing on my mind. Plus, my then-husband John placed zero emphasis on my outer beauty, so neither did I. Because of these factors, I never attempted to do *anything* to make me feel sexy or confident.

When my husband and I started dating, I didn't own makeup, jewelry, perfume, sexy clothing, or shoes that had soles higher than one inch. But ever so slowly and delicately, he expressed the enjoyment and excitement he receives when his partner looks sexy by the type of clothing, jewelry, etc, she wears. Woah! This would be a tall order for me, but with the thrill of a new partner and the excitement of the Bliss Zone, I made the effort and went far outside my comfort zone. I wanted to impress and please him. It took some time, but I bought lots of sexy clothes, pretty shoes, jewelry, makeup, highlighted my hair, and became a regular at the nail salon.

I went the whole nine yards and found the experience a lot of fun. Although at the beginning of this transformation I felt like a fish out of water, the reaction from him when I put myself together was well worth the effort I was pouring into myself. I have to be honest though, it did feel uncomfortable and unnatural at first, especially because I had never been one to draw attention to myself. But he thoroughly enjoyed my new look and constantly let me know he noticed my efforts. He complimented me like crazy, could not keep his hands off me, and made me feel like I was, in fact, the most beautiful woman in the world.

And guess what his compliments and attention did? They helped build my confidence! He made me feel so sexy and desired, like I was *the bomb*. His constant compliments combined with me loving my new look created the desire to tap deeper into my sexuality. Before this time in my life, I never really felt *sexy*. But experiencing this new energy of what sexiness felt like created a whole new, and wonderful I might add, perception of myself.

When you feel sexy, your sense of sexuality increases, which exudes confidence. It's a simple reverse formula.

Sexy = Confidence
Confidence = Sexy

Plastic Surgery

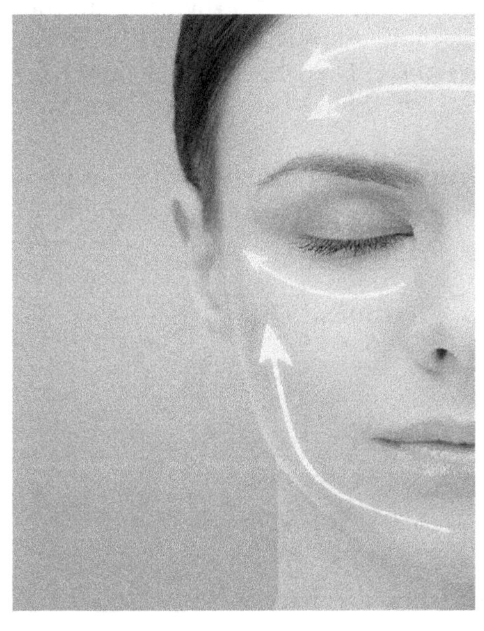

I think it's worthwhile to mention plastic surgery while we're on the subject of confidence. As a woman in our modern world, you have the privilege of deciding if plastic surgery is an avenue you would like to explore.

Many simple, non-surgical procedures can make you feel amazing and give you a boost to feel a little more youthful and *a lot* sexier. I think it's fantastic that women have so many options to choose from nowadays. Minor preventative maintenance procedures such as Botox, fillers, and laser treatments are not cost-prohibitive, so for many women, it has become a viable option to help combat the aging process.

According to the American Society of Plastic Surgeons, over 18 million surgical and minimally invasive cosmetic procedures were performed in 2019. That number is based on procedures in the United States alone. Can you imagine how many procedures are performed annually on women (and men) on a global scale?

I will share with you my experiences with plastic surgery/cosmetic procedures. I had cute and perky boobs back in the pre-children days of my life. However, after breastfeeding my two sons back-to-back for four years straight ***(yes, four years straight)***, well, let's just say my girls went from cute and perky to completely deflated.

Even though I labored to get my physique back after my second son (so I would no longer be mistaken for carrying a third child), I was still awfully self-conscious about this area of my body. I didn't like it, nor did I appreciate what was left *at all.* (This is yet another example of what the female body endures for the thankless job of keeping the human race going strong.)

So anyway, I decided to get breast augmentation after becoming a widow. The timing was intentional because I wanted this decision to be mine and mine alone. I could not be happier with my decision because it boosted my confidence level tremendously.

Now, please do not misconstrue what I am saying. You do not have to spend thousands of dollars on fake boobs to gain confidence. **No. That's not what I'm saying at all.** ***This was my experience.*** It made *me* feel better about *my* outer appearance. Everyone is different, and that's why I must reiterate: it's an entirely individual decision to take whatever steps YOU are comfortable with, if you take any steps at all.

My other experience was a cosmetic procedure. It was a filler-injection on the vertical lines above my upper-lip that my eyes gravitated to every time I looked in the mirror. I loved the results, and I would absolutely do it again. Not only are those lines back, but I now have some quite defined marionette lines too. *Oh, aging process...why won't you just leave me alone?*

Here's the bottom line. If you want to improve your confidence level from where it's at now, then take action to do for yourself whatever *you* believe will make *you* feel the best and most confident version of *you.*

If that means eating healthier and establishing an exercise routine, **do it.**

If that means overhauling your entire wardrobe, **do it.**

If that means trying a different hairstyle, **do it.**

If that means getting a little help from the plastic surgery community, **do it.**

If that means working with your amazing natural beauty, **then do that.**

If that means buying yourself a little treat at the store, that small gesture of self-love counts!

You get my point...

You just have to do ***something!***

Own Your Sexuality

Even though I'm a middle-aged woman and clearly see the signs of aging, I still feel great when I attempt to look good. When I invest the time to make myself look hot and sexy, my husband still gushes over me like a waterfall. I forget about my imperfections and place my focus on feeling sexy, sensual, and confident. I really hope if you take the time to put yourself together nicely, your partner acknowledges your efforts and showers you with compliments too!

Have you ever berated yourself in front of your man? Do you know that when you're critical of yourself within his earshot, it's unappealing to him? This verbal abuse you inflict upon yourself doesn't say "confidence," which almost every man on the planet enjoys in a woman. Believe me when I say, when you point out every flaw to him, he is *not* interested in hearing you beat yourself up.

When he looks at you, he's not looking *at* your imperfections, nor is he looking *for* your imperfections. He is looking at the beauty of his woman. When he tries to convince you of your beauty but is only met with negative replies, it makes him feel bad. *Really bad.* If you're in the habit of doing what I just described, please stop. It's not productive for either of you. Bite your tongue, zip your lip, and thank him for the sweet compliments.

If you concentrate your energy on reconnecting to your sexuality, this energy can flow into a change for the better in your relationship. Focus on what you love and admire about yourself instead of putting yourself down, being critical of yourself, or concentrating on imperfections.

Some final thoughts on confidence…

I'm a true believer that ultimately what makes a woman authentically beautiful is her inner beauty, which she then projects outward. Your personal goal for this key is to begin aligning your inner and outer beauty. You are a beautiful soul on the inside, so allow that beauty to shine through on the outside for all to enjoy...including yourself. If you struggle with insecurity or low self-worth, if you're self-conscious or have no self-esteem, this type of energy flows from you like a mighty river. But there's great news...if you choose to believe you are sexy, sensuous, beautiful, desired, and overall amazing, that type of energy will flow from you in the very same way.

Be gentle, kind, and compassionate with yourself and let go of self-criticism. The human body goes through a tremendous amount of change throughout our lives. Regardless of your appearance today or whether you would like to make any changes, embrace your body, and simply love and accept every square inch. Try not to beat yourself up. Not a single person out of eight billion who reside on this planet is perfect. NOT ONE.

You are beautiful. Believe it. Celebrate your womanhood and your sexuality. Learn to accept flaws that are a part of you and change the flaws you can if they make you feel bad. Choose to be the woman who exudes confidence. You are what you believe, so believe you are a sexual goddess and act like one. Open yourself up and connect to her. (Yes, she is in there!) Then follow up your belief by making the effort to show yourself, your partner, and the world what a confident, sexy, and beautiful woman you are.

Honest Assessment

1. On a scale from 1 to 10, how confident do you feel today and why?

2. On a scale from 1 to 10, how would you rank your self-esteem and why?

3. What type of energy do you exude: confidence or insecurity? Why?

4. Do you have a healthy or poor body image? If it's poor, why do you suppose that's true? If it's healthy, what are some things you've done to contribute to that feeling?

5. When you're out of the house alone, shopping or running errands, do you notice men look at you or do you feel invisible?

____

____

____

6. Do you leave the house looking nicely put together or do you throw on anything, pull your hair back, and not give much thought about your appearance?

____

____

____

7. How often do you have sexually related thoughts?

____

____

____

8. Do you feel detached from your sexual goddess? If so, why? If not, what have you done to stay connected to her?

____

____

____

9. If you could do one thing today to give your confidence a boost, what would it be?

____

____

____

Sexercise: Enjoy a Self(ie) Day!

- ✓ Start this *Self(ie) Day* by taking a nice morning walk around the most scenic nearby area. Think about how important it is to care for yourself and carve out "me time" in your busy schedule. When you get back to your house, eat a light breakfast of fresh tropical fruit and citrus water. What a wonderful way to start the day!
- ✓ You've already made an appointment to get a facial or body massage (maybe even both), so hop in the shower, shave your legs, and get ready to enjoy a wonderfully self-indulgent spa experience.
- ✓ Treatment(s) complete. Now head over to the nail salon for a mani/pedi. You've already relaxed at the spa, and now your fingers and toes look *oh so pretty*. Good for you! You're starting to feel good, but you scold yourself for taking so long to treat yourself and vow to somehow make this a routine event, as you should.
- ✓ Time for a nice, light, healthy bite to eat for lunch, because I want you to keep feeling good. Eating healthy just feels smart!
- ✓ After lunch, go to your favorite clothing store and pick out at least one sexy and flattering outfit. Your shopping goal is to put together a complete outfit from head to toe. While shopping, keep your mindset on *sexy*. Think hot, think form-fitting, think *Damn, I'm going to look goood* or *My man will love this on me.* Don't neglect to buy a sexy bra and underwear set. It will be a let-down if you're looking fine on the outside, but he finds your tattered underwear and old bra underneath all that new sexy goodness. Choose sexy wear that flatters your best assets and "fixes" problem areas. Don't be afraid to ask for assistance with bra sizing. Choose something that makes you feel sexy and in line with what your partner loves.
- ✓ Buy a new fragrance you'll both enjoy, either perfume or a lightly fragrant body lotion.
- ✓ On your way home from this special day, treat yourself to a fancy Starbucks drink. Somehow, it feels ultra-sophisticated to spend $6 on a beverage.

Consider inviting a good friend along on your *Self(ie) Day*. Explain to her the purpose of this day filled with gestures to spoil yourself, and who knows? Maybe your efforts will make her check her confidence level and sexual intimacy status in her own relationship.

The point of this special day is to jolt yourself back to what's important, and that is to ***focus on yourself, take care of yourself, and feel good about yourself.*** I hope you feel deserving of this wonderful day intended to make you feel relaxed and rejuvenated. Carving out intentional time and pampering yourself is a beautiful and kind gift of self-love.

Whenever possible, give your new outfit a trial run complete with hair and makeup. Do everything you would do to get ready as if you were planning to unveil the *new you* to your man. Now stand before that full-length mirror for a ***selfie session!*** Don't be shy! Draw on your inner Kardashian—she's in there! Enjoy your new look! Get excited by how awesome you feel and have fun! There's a good chance those pictures might even make it to your social media accounts. And why not? Isn't that what those accounts are for anyway? Sharing photos and making or seeking compliments? I bet you'll get some flattering comments, which will boost your confidence another notch.

Decide when you will reveal the sexy *new you* to your partner. Here are two ways to execute this: You can surprise him by cooking a nice dinner at home, and he can find you all dressed up and looking amazing for him when he gets home (kids at the sitters, please), or you can go out to dinner. I've also suggested in your Sexercise for Key Six: Dance of Seduction, an opportune time to wear your new outfit. Believe me, regardless of where you go or what you do, those details will be secondary. More than anything else, he will be thrilled by the effort you made to look pretty for him.

Note: If you are unable to fulfill this Self(ie) Day because of financial restrictions, not to worry! Here's an outline of a more cost-effective way to spend your special day.

- ✓ Enjoy a morning walk in nature. This is one of the most soul-nurturing experiences, and it doesn't cost a dime.
- ✓ You don't have to buy fancy tropical fruit for breakfast to enjoy a healthy fruit bowl. You can buy a banana, apple, and orange for less than $3. Take a slice of orange for your citrus water.
- ✓ Find a local massage school for a reduced-priced massage or facial. If that's not an option, buy a new nail polish, give yourself a manicure, and go to a nail salon for a professional pedicure, which includes a lower leg and foot massage. (Take your nail polish so your fingers and toes match.) Or go to a technical college to get a mani/pedi for reduced-priced services.
- ✓ If none of those scenarios work-out, buy a new nail polish, which should cost less than $4, and give yourself a mani/pedi.
- ✓ For your health-conscious lunch, you can whip together a salad for less than $5. You probably have half the ingredients in your fridge already.
- ✓ You don't have to break the bank for your new outfit! Consignment shops are filled with quality, high-end clothing and shoes for a fraction of retail cost. There's also stores like TJ Maxx, Marshalls, and Ross that carry reduced-priced clothing and shoes. And don't neglect to check out the clearance racks while shopping! You should be able to put together a nice outfit including shoes for less than $30, if you shop smart.

- ✓ Bras and underwear are inexpensive at the stores I just mentioned, and by the way, don't knock stores like Target and Walmart. They carry large selections of bras and underwear. It's doubtful your man will know the difference between a $12 set from Target versus a $50 set from Victoria Secret. He'll just be excited to see you wearing something sexy and new!
- ✓ Swing by a department store like Macy's and sample the perfume. You can ask the sales associate for a sample of your favorite fragrance. Sample = FREE!
- ✓ While Dunkin Donuts doesn't carry the same *je ne sais quoi* as Starbucks, most DD stores have happy-hour prices in the afternoon, so you can still enjoy a fancy-like drink for around $2.

This inexpensive version of your *Self(ie) Day* should fall in the price range of $50 (or up to $80, if you include a spa treatment).

My SIM Journal

Write about your ***Self(ie) Day.*** How did you feel overall on your special day? Did you feel deserving of the much-needed self-love and attention you showered upon yourself? Or did you feel guilty that you spent time and money on yourself? Did your confidence boost when you saw yourself in the mirror looking pretty? Did looking amazing create the motivation to take time to spend on yourself more often? When you revealed your sexy look to your partner, what was his reaction?

You don't have to stop here…and you shouldn't. Keep the momentum going! Make a list of the ways you will continue to care about yourself and keep your confidence level at the higher end of the spectrum. Make a self-promise to move yourself up on your priority list and stick to that promise!

The Key to Confidence!

The key to confidence is your state of mind. How you perceive yourself internally will be expressed outwardly, and others will pick up your vibe. Be mindful of what you choose to express to your partner, yourself, and to the public at large.

KEY FOUR
Self-Exploration

Do you remember a long, long time ago before the first boy ever laid hands on you? You experienced new sensations as your female body parts began to blossom. Naturally, curiosity gave way to self-exploration. Masturbation. This is most likely how you learned what felt good to you, how to pleasure yourself and most importantly, how to give yourself an orgasm.

I remember when I arrived at pubescence. I began to experience an unfamiliar tingling in my vagina. *Where was this sensation coming from?* I was compelled to investigate, and it became a personal challenge to see if I could intensify this feeling. However, this challenge was easier said than done. I don't know if you were lucky enough to have your own childhood bedroom, but unfortunately, I wasn't. I shared a room with one of my sisters, so it was difficult to explore without the luxury of true privacy.

Since my bedroom was off-limits because my sister always seemed to be around, I became very resourceful in my quest for self-exploration around the house. I rubbed my vagina against any inanimate object every chance I could, all the while making sure not to get caught. The arm of the couch, stuffed animals, the end-corner of a bed, my pillow. I even figured out a way to manipulate my lower leg so I could pleasure myself that way too–oh, clever and flexible me! What a sight that must have been! Oh, to be a fly on the wall.

I even remember doing Kegel exercises in my classes at school, not realizing what they were and the benefits of them. I just knew it felt good to flex those inner muscles. The only time I explored myself with my fingers was at night when the lights were out. Although, I hardly ever tried because I felt too paranoid with my sister in the room. Come to find out later in life, she played with herself, nightly. I guess she wasn't overly concerned about me!

Self-exploration during puberty is so natural and such an important part of learning how to connect to your body. Eventually, this innate curiosity becomes satisfied through sexual exploration with another person, so the need naturally lessens over time to continue exploring and satisfying yourself.

Well, my friend, it's time to venture into this territory again. Not as a curious young girl, but as a seasoned woman. At the end of this chapter, you will find several opportunities to become reacquainted with your body through some great ways to reintroduce self-exploration back into your life.

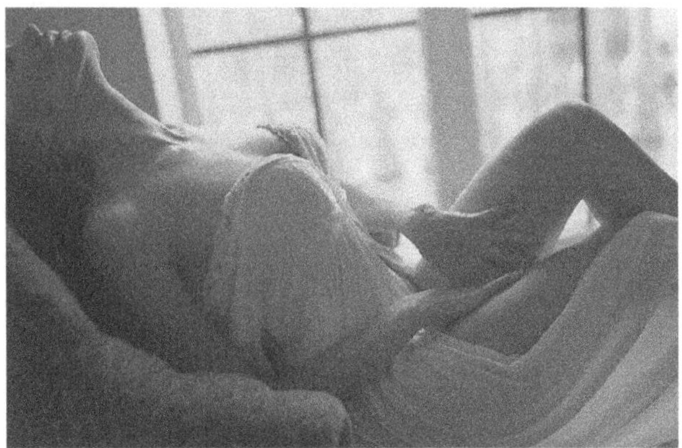

Do you still feel connected to your body? Or did you lose connection a long time ago? I'm talking about on any level, not just sexually. If you have lost touch with your body, it's rather difficult to summon the sexual goddess within because you're no longer connected to her. You've allowed her to go on a hiatus. It's virtually impossible to feel sexual and sensual when you're not in touch with her, so you *must* find her and reconnect with her.

Do you partake in any of the following activities to stay connected to yourself on a physical level? Checkmark all that apply:

- ☐ Exercise regularly
- ☐ Practice yoga
- ☐ Meditation
- ☐ Breathing techniques
- ☐ Massages/facials
- ☐ Masturbation (with/without toys)
- ☐ Preventative/annual health checkups
- ☐ Take vitamins/supplements
- ☐ Eat healthy
- ☐ Enjoy outdoor physical activities
- ☐ Overall, maintain a strong body awareness

If you currently do not use any of these methods to stay in touch with your body, consider incorporating some of them into your life. Be mindful that your physical body is a temple that houses your beautiful soul. Your temple is precious and should be treated as such.

Here's a perfect example of how easily a person can lose touch with their body if they're not paying attention. Years ago, my sisters and I went on an amazing tropical vacation together. One beautiful, sunny morning, the four of us took a beach yoga class. While holding the last pose, one of my sisters burst out crying. Perplexed and concerned, we gathered around and asked why she was upset. She explained she was overwhelmed by how disconnected she felt from her body.

This was a woman who had entered many bodybuilding competitions and always kept herself in stellar physical shape. However, after three children and 15 years of a strained marriage, a major disconnect had occurred without her realizing it. That is, until that morning yoga class. Struggling with the yoga poses immediately brought to her attention just how much she had lost touch with her body.

If you're in a similar situation, this disconnect can affect your life in significant ways such as your general health, sexuality, confidence level, and the bond of intimacy with your partner. For all these reasons, the physical connection to your body is too important to let go. That said, this part of the journey is about reconnecting to your physical being. We will work on closing the gap that may have grown over time with your body, and work on improving your physical relationship with your partner as well. There is a very good chance he's more than ready to rebuild the bond of sexual intimacy with you and has been a willing participant all along. If you work on reconnecting with your body through different methods of self-exploration, you will have a greater chance of this reconnection manifesting itself in positive ways in your relationship.

Honest Assessment

1. Have you lost touch with your body? How so?

2. In which ways, if any, have you remained connected?

3. When was the last time you physically exerted yourself?

4. How would you rank your eating habits? If they are poor, do you have the desire to improve them?

EXCELLENT / AVERAGE / POOR

5. When was the last time you masturbated? Did you orgasm?

6. If you masturbate routinely, is it out of sexual dissatisfaction?

____

____

____

7. Has your partner ever watched you play with yourself?

YES / NO

8. Have you ever played with yourself specifically to please him?

YES / NO

9. What elements are you willing to add to your life to improve the physical connection to yourself? (i.e., exercise, massages, meditation)

____

____

____

Sexercise One: Reconnect Visually And Physically To Your Body

In this first of four Sexercises, you will focus on reconnecting to your body. When you have about 30 minutes of alone time (yes, I know that's a joke, but try), lock yourself in your bedroom and stand naked, in all your glory, before a full-length mirror. Do this after showering and shaving your legs (it feels so much better for the second part of this Sexercise).

Start from the top of your head and scan every inch of your body. Make mental notes of everything you see about your body you feel happy with or think is beautiful. Don't skip a single attribute. If you like a particular freckle on your cheek, take note. During your self-scan, acknowledge the body parts you consider imperfect, but don't criticize yourself about these perceived flaws. Observe without judgment.

Be mindful; don't pick yourself apart, be harsh, or criticize your body during this Sexercise. Be gentle and compassionate as you perform this self-assessment. I understand this can be tricky because innately, we want to attack ourselves when it comes to our imperfections. The key is to see yourself from *outside* of yourself. You must drop your ego momentarily and look at your body as if you are looking at your best friend's body. You should speak to yourself as if you were encouraging a loved one away from their insecurities. We're all naturally attached to our self-identities, but the more we can drop them, the more we can dispel illusions, i.e., the idea that we have anything less than beautiful bodies.

The purpose of this Sexercise is for you to reconnect with your body in a visually positive way. Embrace your body exactly the way it looks today and accept it with compassion. Look into your eyes and tell yourself with sincerity you love who you are and how you look...*flaws and all.* Then give yourself a nice, big bear hug!

You will now take this Sexercise a step further and begin the physical reconnection.

Grab a towel and some lotion, powder, or oil. Instead of standing in the bathroom and haphazardly slopping it on your body, feeling hurried to get to the next thing, take your time. Make this everyday, uneventful task an intentional and sensual experience to reconnect with your body. Please make time for this...it's worth it.

Bring your after-shower product and towel to the bed. Sit on your towel with your legs stretched in front of you. Now squeeze out some product and rub your hands together, then apply slowly, gently, and intentionally to one section of your body at a time. Start with your feet, move to your calves, and then your thighs. When you're done with your lower half, lay down with your head propped up slightly on a pillow or two. Continue with each arm, neck, chest, breasts, and finally your stomach. Do not allow your hands to travel between your legs. That area will be addressed right around the corner.

Perform this Sexercise either looking at your body or with closed eyes. I suggest trying both ways. Enjoy what you're watching and then close your eyes to tap deeper into your sense of touch. Take your time and tenderly caress the sweet-smelling product into each part of your body. Experiment by using a lighter touch, then a firmer touch. Compare what feels good to what feels awesome. Explore your body and enjoy the feelings you experience. Stay completely present while practicing this Sexercise. Listen to relaxing spa music and light a deliciously fragrant candle. Why not? Experience as many pleasant, sensory sensations as possible.

Sexercise Two: Reconnect To Your Health And Wellbeing

Do you exercise? Or can you not even remember the last time you put on sneakers to physically exert yourself? Most people have jumped on the exercise bandwagon and jumped right back off. If you currently practice a healthy lifestyle, that's fantastic! You're ahead of the game, so keep up the great work! However, if you're like many women with a limited amount of time in their daily schedule, it can be easy to justify sacrificing your health. This thought process is totally unacceptable. Your health is the last thing you should sacrifice! When you have taken time for yourself to work out and make healthy food choices (because they usually go hand in hand), how do you feel? And when you choose not to partake in any physical fitness or make the best food choices, how do you feel?

I've been on both sides of this ever-flipping coin. When I make exercise and eating healthy a priority, I feel smart because I know I'm making healthy choices. I also feel more confident because I'm investing time and energy into transforming my body into the way I most enjoy seeing it. I also feel more energetic and lighter because I'm choosing to nourish my body with healthier food choices.

However, when I neglect my body, I feel consumed with guilt knowing I'm not honoring my body how I should. I don't feel smart, because I understand a sedentary lifestyle is not reflective of good health. Nor do I feel confident because I'm self-conscious about my muffin top or about the over-abundance of cellulite on my legs, butt, and even my arms! I also feel lazy and lethargic and plain old *blah* because I'm not fueling my body with nutritious food. I'm filling it with junk food, which makes me feel horrible both emotionally and physically.

Undoubtedly, if you live healthily, you will feel smarter, more confident, more energetic, and downright sexier. And you don't have to be a size 4 to achieve what I mean. The key is to make healthy food choices and to get your body in physical motion to improve your overall health.

That said, I want you to create an exercise routine. Yes, that's right! Make a commitment to improve your health. Start slowly. If you never exercise, begin physical activity once a week. Make sure it's on the same day and time so you form a routine. If you don't exercise, start out the right way and get a physical. Let your doctor give you the thumbs-up for what he feels you can handle in your current physical state. If you already have a workout routine, take it to the next level and do it more often, or try different physical activities. For example, if you only workout at a gym, try an outdoor activity.

Consider activities like tennis, golf, swimming, kayaking, bicycling, hiking, rock climbing, yoga, weightlifting, racquetball, kickboxing, or aerobic classes. It's essential to choose an activity you'll enjoy. This way, you will look forward to the activity and want to do it more often. Don't pick an activity you'll dread because you won't stay interested. Give it some thought and choose something you've always wanted to try or pick up again.

My personal favorite exercises are walking, yoga, belly-dancing, and Zumba classes. I thoroughly enjoy these exercises because not only is my body in motion, but I also feel joy in my heart and experience a sense of release when I'm doing them. It's a win-win!

Whatever activity you choose, don't feel self-conscious or unsure about learning a physical activity that's unfamiliar. Learning a new skill takes time, so be patient with the process. If you join a gym and want to take an aerobics class, don't let feelings of intimidation stop you. Everyone in that class looked slightly uncoordinated or moved to a different beat on their first day. *Who cares?* No one will pay attention or pass judgment because they've all been there too.

If you find it too difficult to muster the courage to go alone, persuade a friend to take the class with you. You'll have both an accountability partner *and* a security blanket. Besides, after a few weeks, you'll have mastered the routine so well and feel so confident in your abilities, you'll think to yourself that you could be the back-up instructor if your teacher were to ever get stuck in traffic and not make it to class on time!

On days you exercise, skip the donut party at the office and fast food for lunch. Eat a bowl of fresh fruit for breakfast and a tuna, turkey, or veggie wrap for lunch instead. Substitute one of your sugary and caffeinated drinks for a bottle of water. Take baby steps and before long, you'll feel better because you're being kind to your body, which is exactly what it craves.

Whatever you do...do *not* unnecessarily pressure yourself by focusing on your current weight and how many pounds you want to lose. Weight loss isn't the purpose of this Sexercise. It's important not to gauge your journey to better health based on a number the scale pops out, and then allow that number to dictate how you feel. Let your good choices determine how you feel. If you attempt to improve your health on any level, be proud of the effort you're making. If you lose some weight because of your healthier choices, fabulous! But again, weight loss isn't the focus of this Sexercise.

Remember, anytime the body is in motion, no matter what motion...it's a good thing! Speaking of moving your body, consider adding some physical exercise on your bed. Here's a list of the top ten benefits of a horizontal workout.

Ten Health Benefits of Sex

1. Improved Immunity

People who have sex frequently (1-2 times a week) have significantly higher levels of immunoglobulin, which is your body's first line of defense to fight off invading organisms.

2. Heart Health

Sexual activity keeps levels of estrogen and testosterone in balance, which is important for heart health.

3. Lower Blood Pressure

Sexual activity is linked to better stress response and lower blood pressure.

4. Form of Exercise

Sex boosts your heart rate, burns calories, and strengthens muscles. Recent research reveals sex burns about 4 calories per minute for men and 3 calories per minute for women, making it a legitimate form of exercise. Sex can also help maintain flexibility and balance.

5. Pain Relief

Sexual activity releases pain-reducing hormones. It reduces or blocks back and leg pain, menstrual cramp pain, arthritis, and headaches. One study found that sexual activity can lead to partial or complete relief in some migraine and cluster headache patients.

6. Improved Sleep

After sex, the relaxation-inducing hormone prolactin releases, which may help you fall asleep more quickly. When you orgasm, the hormone oxytocin releases, which also promotes sleep.

7. Stress Relief

Sex triggers your body to release its natural feel-good chemicals, which helps ease stress and boost pleasure, calmness, and self-esteem. Research also shows those who are active sexually respond better when subjected to stressful situations like speaking in public.

8. Boost Your Libido

The more often you have sex, the more likely you are to want to keep having sex. There's a mental connection, but also a physical one, particularly for women. Having sex more frequently helps increase vaginal lubrication, blood flow, and elasticity, leading to more enjoyable sex.

9. Improved Bladder Control

Having sex helps strengthen your pelvic floor muscles, which contract during orgasm. This can help women improve their bladder control and avoid incontinence. You can boost this benefit by practicing Kegel exercises during sex (your man will highly appreciate this exercise routine) or even when sitting at your desk at work. (Wouldn't your boss love to know that little detail?)

10. Increase Intimacy and Improve Your Relationship

Sex and orgasms result in increased levels of the hormone oxytocin, the love hormone, which increases intimate bonding and empathy.

* * *

People occasionally ask what my exercise routine is because I still have a decent figure at my age. If I'm asked that question during a period of physical inactivity, I say, "Oh, not much really. I exercise whenever I get the chance, but I'm not in a set routine right now." Meanwhile, I giggle to myself because what I really want to say is, "Well actually, I work out multiple times a week in my bed with my husband." But I refrain, smile politely, and thank them for the compliment.

Sex is a great physical workout and can really get the blood pumping through your body. Even if you miss your chance to exercise during the day, there's always a workout opportunity waiting in your bed if you still want to get your sweat on. The great part is that you have a workout partner to help motivate you!

Sexercise Three: Reconnect To Your Sexual Energy

This Sexercise focuses on sexually exploring your body, which can heighten desire for your partner. When was the last time you played with yourself? Was it out of necessity because you and your partner aren't so active anymore? Or because sex is over so quick there's no time to orgasm? Was it because you felt horny out-of-the-blue and wanted to relieve yourself? Or do you not even try because your vagina has gone dormant from inactivity?

As discussed at the beginning of this chapter, most teenagers begin their sexual journey through self-exploration, long before the experience of sexual activity with another person. Masturbation is typically the gateway into the world of sexuality. It's done out of curiosity and the desire to experience pleasure.

As you've gotten older, maybe the need to keep in touch with your body has diminished. However, it's important from time to time to pleasure yourself. Not only does it feel good, but it also keeps you in touch with your body on a sexual level. When you can seize a moment, prepare for this Sexercise by finding a soft blanket to lie on, grab a hand towel to put under your butt, lock your bedroom door, and close the curtains. Be sure you have a silky soft personal lubricant or organic massage oil to rub on your vagina. Pull out your vibrator of choice, or if you don't have one (shame on you), please buy one immediately! And you always have your trusty fingers as an option.

Enjoy yourself. Explore yourself. Excite yourself.

Fully immerse yourself in the moment and revel in the sensations you feel in and around your vaginal area. Use your vibrator or fingers to stimulate your clitoris until you're close to climaxing, but then stop as many times as you can before you allow yourself the pleasure of a full orgasm. In other words, tease yourself. However, if you can orgasm multiple times during self-pleasure sessions, then have at it! Masturbation is a wonderful way to rouse your sexual desire, which can have a positive effect on renewing a good sexual relationship with your partner.

Fourth And Final Sexercise: *Ooooh…This One's A Biggie!* Give Each Other A Show

Ask your man if he wants to enjoy a hot and steamy shower with you. Assuming he says yes, because I can't imagine he wouldn't, grab the body wash and lather him up the same way you lathered yourself with your after-shower product in the first Sexercise. Then lather yourself seductively, starting with your upper body. Whatever parts of your body he loves most, place your focus on those areas. Play with yourself for him and encourage him to play with himself while he's watching you. Don't feel shy or embarrassed to give him a show. Trust me, he will go crazy with excitement!

These four Sexercises will help you reconnect to yourself physically, so you can begin the process of reawakening sexual desire for your partner. The time has come to be the playful, amorous, and sexy woman you once were and are more than capable of becoming once again.

My SIM Journal

If you can remember, write in your journal about your first experiences with self-exploration during your youth. Can you plug into the feelings of curiosity and physical excitement you felt way back when? Write how you experienced those new sexual sensations and how they made your body feel.

Then write about your experience with each Sexercise. Were they pleasurable or did they feel awkward to you? Did they make you feel a renewed sense of connection to your body? Did you notice if a disconnection happened over time, like it did for my sister? List some goals for staying physically connected to yourself.

The Key to Self-Exploration

The key to self-exploration is making intentional time to explore and enjoy your body. Becoming more closely in tune and actively seeking new ways to stay connected to yourself physically can increase your sexual desire. By default, this can benefit your relationship through increased sexual intimacy with your partner.

KEY FIVE
Affection and Bonding

It's Friday night. You and your man decide to relax with a movie after a long and crazy week. Once you've grabbed a drink and popcorn from the kitchen, you head to the living room and situate yourself on the couch. Where do you sit?

A. Your favorite spot on the couch. You each have a bowl of popcorn, so it doesn't matter where he sits.

B. You sit close enough to him so you can reach into the bowl and share the popcorn, but not right next to him.

C. You sit right next to each other and the bowl is on his lap (he calculatingly places it there so he can get a thrill every time your hand moves towards his groin area to get more popcorn).

D. Your body is draped across his body in some way, shape, or form. Who cares where the popcorn is?

E. Movie? *What movie?* You can't even remember the last time you sat down to watch a movie together.

Well, what's your answer? Are you holding it down in the affection department or do you have some work to do?

Affection is one way, especially at the beginning of a relationship, we show adoration for the other person. To give and receive affection makes us feel good, special, and loved. Remember the Bliss Zone? Would you agree it was effortless to dole out endless kisses and hugs, walk arm-in-arm or hold hands in public, and lovingly massage his neck and shoulders after a hard day's work? How about all those sweet nothings and compliments you showered upon him like a daily rainstorm?

I bet you can't count how many special dinners you prepared or the number of cards you bought him...*just because.* Do you remember when it was impossible to go shopping without grabbing his favorite snack or drink? You were exceptionally affectionate and thoughtful while in the Bliss Zone, and you lived to make your man feel special and loved. These verbal, physical, and thoughtful gestures conveyed how much you cared about his happiness. It seems fair to ask this question since you're reading this guide: Do you remember the last time you showed him any of these expressions of love?

Affection is an extremely important bond that keeps long-term relationships energized. If you stop showing affection (even though you still love him), he will naturally feel unloved and unwanted. Think about what an unspoken gesture affection is. It says, "I love you," wordlessly. When affection dries up, it's as though you stop saying those three small but powerful words.

So, has the once flowing river of affection slowed to a mere trickle? Although a BIG mistake, it's very common in long-term relationships. Yet not every couple makes this mistake. I'm sure you've seen those adorable elderly couples walking arm-in-arm, still showing each other affection after all their years together. I have, and it melts my heart every time. They understand the importance of keeping the bond of affection strong. When you see them, admire them, and be inspired to maintain that same special bond in your relationship.

One of my past relationships was with a guy who wasn't holding it down in the affection department. Well, let me clarify...he wasn't affectionate, period. I didn't pay much attention at the beginning because I was so focused and excited about the sexual aspect of our relationship. But as time went by, the lack of affection outside the bedroom became glaringly obvious. We had a large sectional couch in our living room and when he came home from work, he would sit as far away from me as possible. No kiss hello, no hug, no physical acknowledgment. I don't think he once sat next to me or, God forbid, put his arm around my shoulder. There was simply no affection, ever. I honestly don't think he was intentionally neglectful or unaffectionate, but that actually felt even more disheartening. Affection wasn't part of his upbringing, and unfortunately, that missing link persisted into his adult life.

I *longed* for affection. I craved to feel a loving and caring touch. But for him, it was awkward... he just wasn't capable. I repeatedly explained my strong need for affection and did everything in my power to convey how much I needed this missing piece in our relationship. Because he couldn't show me love in this way, his lack of affection made me feel rejected and unloved. As time went on, it became increasingly difficult to deal with the constant emptiness and feelings of loneliness. In fact, the issue became so big, it ultimately ended our relationship. I decided I'd rather be single and alone than be with someone and feel lonely.

I'm happy to say after 13 years together, my current relationship is filled with loving and affectionate gestures. On the bed, off the bed, it doesn't matter. Between the two of us, Angel is the one who remains mindful of our level of affection. I admit, I'm guilty of getting swept up in the everyday grind. There have been times I've forgotten to kiss him hello when I come home on exceptionally hectic or stressful days. It's unintentional, but if my mind is scattered in 17 different directions, I'm just not thinking about it. Not until he brings it to my attention, that is.

As you can see, I've experienced polar opposite scenarios regarding affection in two of my relationships, and the difference is unbelievable. I'm beyond thankful Angel is so tuned into the importance of keeping this bond strong. As long as there's one person in the relationship monitoring the affection gauge who gently reminds the other person when it drops, I feel that's acceptable. The real problem begins when *no one* is paying attention and before you know it, you are friends (or enemies) with occasional benefits.

Typically, there will be one person who is more affectionate by nature, but that doesn't mean they should carry all the weight. No scenario will ever work well if only one person is making all the effort. Assess the current level of affection in your relationship. Who's working hard to keep it alive? If it's him, become more mindful and make a stronger effort. If it's you, communicate how important affection is so he can step up his game. If it's neither, then you both have your work cut out!

No matter how many years go by, maintaining the bond of affection is the glue that holds the relationship together. Undeniably, it takes more effort as time goes on, but without affection, what do you have? A roommate? What fun is that? Stop for a minute and think about your interactions. Are they dull, dry, and lifeless? Or warm, affectionate, and playful?

You're still with this man and have some investment in your relationship; otherwise, you wouldn't be reading this guide. Even if it feels a little uncomfortable at first (and it probably will), why not attempt to turn this part of your relationship around?

I can't stress the importance of affection enough because it's such an integral component of a healthy and fulfilling long-term relationship. To drive my point further, here's an analogy related to the importance of maintaining affection with your partner and what happens when you don't.

Water the Plant!

You decide you want to buy a beautiful house plant. At the store, you find the perfect plant—a lush Monstera with those big, heart-shaped leaves. When you bring it home, you place it in the best room for proper lighting. You carefully transplant it into a beautiful pot, water it religiously, fertilize it so it can grow nice and lush, and keep the leaves dust-free and shiny. You even talk to it with love. You carefully nurture your new plant, and because you're so attentive to its needs, it flourishes into a thriving, healthy, big and beautiful plant.

Now enter a different reality. You have the same desire to buy a beautiful house plant. You bring the same plant home, but you stick it wherever you think it looks best, regardless of what type of lighting condition it requires. You water it sporadically, forget to fertilize it, and you never talk to it. How do you think the plant will fare? Probably not so good. As a matter of fact, it will eventually die from neglect.

The same principle applies to affection in your relationship. When you both attentively show and give love, this exchange keeps your bond of love solid, strong, and healthy. However, when you drop the effort to nurture this important bond, unfortunately, it will slowly fade. Over time, many other parts of the relationship will follow suit.

You must nourish your relationship with constant TLC, just like the plant. If you're not, get the metaphorical watering can out of the shed, grab some fertilizer, and start bringing life back to your relationship, immediately!

Affection and Sexual Intimacy

The relevance of keeping affection alive is twofold. First, it's an unspoken language used to convey love, which makes your partner feel adored. Second, it's an important element to keep the bond of sexual intimacy strong. How do you typically begin a sexual interaction? Do you start by gently kissing, which turns into passionate kissing? Do you rub and caress each other to create a buildup of excitement? Or do you simply roll over, raise your backside in the air and assume the doggy position, without even a kiss to get warmed up?

Think about these different examples. Kissing, rubbing, and touching creates a buildup of anticipation and excitement. These are important elements in a good sexual interaction. But if none of these elements exist, how else can you get aroused before sex? Don't you need *something* to get your juices flowing? You can't turn that thing on like a water faucet...not like you used to anyway. Affection plays a HUGE role in a good sex life. Showing love and tenderness during the act of sex can make for some amazing sexual experiences together, long after the initial freshness has worn away.

The Triple A's
Appreciation. Acknowledgment. Attention.

We often overlook these three little gems, but when these simple forms of verbal affection are put into play, they can create significant, instantaneous improvements. We're only talking about words here, but do you have any idea how powerful heartfelt verbal affection can be?

Appreciation

Most men have a strong need to feel appreciated. However, few men articulate this need to their partner. Many men feel under-appreciated or flat-out unappreciated for their contribution to the relationship, family, and house-hold. Is it possible your partner may feel unappreciated for everything he does? Even though he has many responsibilities on his plate, that doesn't mean he wouldn't appreciate some verbal gratitude and recognition from you.

One day, when he gets home from work, greet him at the front door and tell him with complete sincerity, "Honey, I really appreciate what a hardworking man you are and what a good provider you are for our family. I'm so grateful for you." Or say, "I want to let you know how much I appreciate it when you take the kids to their sports practices" or "I appreciate it when you tuck the kids in bed at night. I know they love when you spend time with them, and I think you're a wonderful father." Watch him melt. Now and then, think of something you appreciate that he does and let him know.

Acknowledgment

I don't know your partner, but I'll go out on a limb and assume he's like every other man on the planet and enjoys acknowledgment for good deeds and behavior. Do you acknowledge your partner when he helps with the kids without being told, or cleans the kitchen after dinner on his own accord? Or let's say he's trying to quit a bad habit. Do you show compassion and tell him you understand what a big deal breaking a habit can be and how hard it must be for him? If he's attempting to make changes for the better, you MUST let him know you see his efforts by encouraging him. Be his cheerleader and acknowledge the positive changes he's trying to make.

If he fixes something around the house, mows the lawn, or cleans the gutters, acknowledge that he did a great job! *Tell him* you think he's an awesome partner and you're the luckiest woman in the world. Validation from YOU is the biggest motivational force behind his determination to work hard on whatever it is he's trying to accomplish. Validate him!

Attention

When a boy wants attention from a parent, he'll do whatever it takes to get some, am I right? Good or bad, he could care less. At the end of the day, all he wants is attention. Do you think men are much different? My answer is a firm NO. Men love receiving attention and being doted over. Naturally, most men prefer attention that makes them feel good, but ultimately, they'll take whatever they can get. If you ignore your partner, does he act like a jerk or look for a fight? Or if you pay extra attention to him, compliment him on how good he looks, or that his new haircut looks great, aren't you met with a super nice fella?

Most men are driven by their egos, and those little monsters love being fed. Pick a morning before he goes off to work and give his hungry ego a little something to chew on for the day. "Wow honey, you're looking quite handsome today" accompanied by a big hug, some juicy kisses, and maybe even a squeeze on the outside of his pants before you walk away. You've just inflated him to *Superman* status. He'll fly through his day, excited to get back home to his Lois Lane, all for less than ten seconds of your time.

These simple verbal reinforcements of the **Triple A's** can be highly effective in creating feelings of instant happiness in your partner. I hope you speak from a place of honesty, but if you sugarcoat your words a little in the beginning, that's okay. Say them anyway and watch his reaction. It's magical! His whole demeanor will most likely change because you're giving him important affirmations. Moving forward, there's a strong likelihood he'll work even harder on everything he does because he loves the reward. The reward being *appreciation, acknowledgment, and attention*...from you.

Bonding

I don't believe I've ever tried to articulate what it *feels* like to share a bond with someone, but I'll try to find the right descriptive words to explain this type of energy. When a mutual attachment develops between two people, they become surrounded by a powerful energetic barrier that no one or nothing can penetrate. It's such a unique feeling to experience a bond because it's a jointly understood yet unspoken connection. In a romantic relationship, bonding typically happens during the Bliss Zone when two people are in love.

Did you experience a rock-solid bond with your partner once upon a time? If so, did you spend quality time engaging in activities that nurtured this bond? When a couple spends leisure time participating in common interests, a sense of oneness develops and further strengthens this special bond. Unfortunately, as with many elements of a seasoned relationship, fun-filled bonding activities can vanish over time. By default, emotional and intimacy bonds can weaken because remember, all working parts of the relationship are connected.

So, have you maintained any activity bonds to keep you feeling connected? Or have you found new activities to enjoy together? Or as time has passed, have these activities disappeared? If they have, it's beyond common. However, acknowledgment means you're only halfway there. Now the question becomes...what are you going to do about it? You know I've got you covered! I have some fun Sexercises at the end of the chapter for you.

One of my favorite bonding activities I enjoy seeing couples doing together is riding a motorcycle. I think that's *so cool*. Not only because they're riding on a motorcycle and enjoying a fun activity, but I swear, I can feel their bond. There's a strong energy that emanates from them, and I can sense their connection. I don't know how to explain it exactly, but it's an awesome vibe. They share a love for something, and that special bond undoubtedly flows into other areas of their relationship in a positive way.

Now, I'm not saying you have to go buy a motorcycle, wear leather chaps, customize a helmet with skulls and roses, and get a *Born to be Wild* tattoo to have a meaningful bond with your partner. All I'm saying is I admire that bonding activity...it's inspiring!

If you no longer foster friendship bonds that bring out the love, happiness, and good times, then what are you left with? A relationship with only responsibilities? Only problems? Basically, you're left with the grind of life and no enjoyment to accompany the tough stuff. When you actively nurture friendship-type bonding activities and make time to enjoy common interests, you will reap the benefits of a solid and healthy relationship well into your golden years. Continue to cultivate your relationship with enjoyable activities, and who knows? Maybe one day you'll be the king and queen of the shuffleboard court!

Honest Assessment

1. Do you show your partner you love him with physical affection? If so, how? If not, why not?

____

____

____

2. Do you give your partner verbal affection? If so, how? If not, why not?

____

____

____

3. How would you rate the overall affection in your relationship today compared to the beginning? Have you maintained any level of affection or is that area in your relationship a complete drought?

____

____

____

4. What is the exchange that typically leads up to sex?

____

____

____

5. Do you take time to be affectionate with each other before the act of sex itself?

YES / SOMETIMES / NO

6. Do you still kiss throughout your sexual interaction, from beginning to end?

YES / SOMETIMES / NO

7. On average, how often do you tell your man you love him? Do you still compliment him? If so, how often? If not, why not?

8. Does your partner ask you for affection? If so, do you try to step up your efforts? Or are his requests ignored?

9. Do you appreciate, acknowledge, and show him attention? If so, how often? If not, why do you suppose that is?

10. How strong do you feel your overall bond is as a couple? Rate from 1 to 10.

11. Do you have any hobbies/activities you enjoy that maintain your bond? If so, what are they? If not, what are some hobbies/activities you would like to try as a couple?

Sexercise One: *Step It Up!*

It's time to step up your efforts through both physical and verbal affection for this Sexercise. Throughout the week, work on the assignments listed below when you feel moved to say and do them. You may have to remind yourself if you've gotten out of the habit, so be mindful. Set a reminder on your phone if you must. (Sounds funny, but I'm not kidding!)

- ✓ Tell him you love him at least once a day.
- ✓ Give him a nice compliment about anything, once a day.
- ✓ Give him at least one meaningful kiss and hug each day.
- ✓ Show him appreciation, acknowledgment, or attention in some way at least once throughout the week.

The next time you have sex (which I hope will be soon), be extra affectionate at the beginning of your session. Yes, I said session, not a quickie. Sit on top of him, bend down and kiss his neck, ears, chest, and lips before you get into the action. Take your time. This will not only get him highly aroused, but it will hopefully stir up some excitement in you. Set your intention to have an intimate interaction filled with love and affection. I'm sure he'll follow your lead. Men are like puppy dogs. They will inevitably follow no matter which direction you go. And don't forget to kiss, kiss, kiss, and then kiss some more! There's no such thing as too much kissing!

And just a friendly reminder...don't stop the flow of affection after this Sexercise is over. Keep it turned on and continue to increase both physical and verbal affection more and more every day. You won't believe what a renewed sense of love and excitement these gestures can create.

Sexercise Two: Create Or Reintroduce A Bonding Activity

Now is the perfect time in your journey of restoring sexual intimacy to revitalize a bonding activity to bring you closer together. If you didn't have one, find an activity that suits you both.

When you partake in a newfound or once-shared interest, you take an invaluable step towards a stronger relationship. Bonding activities are essential because they create or recreate the opportunity to share happiness, closeness, and fun. In addition, bonding activities are wonderful because they offer the chance to hang out like best friends and forget all the little and big issues that barrage your life. Talk with your partner about what types of bonding activities you would both find enjoyable. And you never know...you might just wind up buying a motorcycle and some leather chaps after all!

In the back section of the guide, you'll find **Sexual Intimacy Ideas.** Look through the **Activity Bonding** section to explore ideas.

My SIM Journal

Write in your journal all the ways you showered each other with physical and verbal affection at the beginning of your relationship. List specific ways you showed thoughtfulness and care towards each other. How did that time make you feel? How do you think it made him feel?

Acknowledge where your level of affection is today, then list what changes you will make for tomorrow. In addition, write about a bonding activity you once enjoyed together (if you did) and relive how that strong connection made you feel.

The Key to Affection and Bonding

The key to open the flow of affection again is to observe your verbal and physical exchanges throughout the day. If neither person is being affectionate, you must take the lead and begin the process.

The key to establish or reestablish a bonding activity with your partner is to PLAN this activity and make it a part of your weekly routine. If you're spontaneous and that works for both of you, great. However, most people have hectic schedules, so it's best to discuss a set day and time to enjoy your bonding activity.

Protect this sacred time and don't let **anything** interfere with this commitment you're making to enjoy special time together. You will witness firsthand how something as simple as a bonding activity can bring the freshness and life back into your relationship.

KEY SIX
Dance of Seduction

Do you remember the evocative dance of seduction? *I know, I know*...it probably feels like an eternity ago—but reminisce for a moment. Do you remember when your relationship was filled with intense feelings of desire overflowing for one another? Suggestive body language? Flirty exchanges? Sexual innuendos? These fun ways of sexual communication created major anticipation and excitement in each other, *for* each other. Tell me. *How exciting was this dance?*

Pause and take a trip down memory lane. Close your eyes and experience the excitement and anticipation you felt during your first year together. You were laser-focused on pleasing each other and constantly engaged in affectionate and playful exchanges. Do you remember all the hot and heavy flirting? Leaving sexy messages? Little surprise love notes? Teasing with naughty texts? Always dressing your absolute best to impress one another? The chemicals were flying and hormones were raging, which made the Bliss Zone of your relationship effortless.

The beginning of a relationship overflows with uncontainable excitement, suggestive and flirtatious gestures, strong sexual energy, and innuendos galore. You might think to yourself, *Why are we even talking about this? Yes, that time was awesome, but that part of our relationship has long since died.* I don't dispute that the flame of flirtation has flickered down significantly, but are you aware of the overall positive effect flirtation has on a relationship? Yes, even in long-term relationships...*especially* in long-term relationships!

Flirtatious behavior is a great way to reignite the spark necessary to rebuild your sexual fire. You might look at him today after so many years together and think, *Eh, he lost that fun and playful side a long time ago...and so have I.* Do not believe that lie! It's still there, it's just gone dormant over the years. You're both still capable of being flirty—everyone is! How many people do you personally know who have come out of long-term relationships, or worse, they go outside the boundary of their current relationship, and they're on fire with their flirtatious behavior?

Imagine you just met your partner and you're interacting with him for the first time. What would your approach be? How hard would you be trying to seduce him with your sex appeal? My guess is there would be a strong effort on your part to make him feel desired. So, my question is this...if you still love him, why not try to make him feel desirable? If you look at your partner with a blank stare and feel nothing stirring inside, you must work on convincing your loins they're on fire for this man. *But how?* Well, you're reading a guide about restoring sexual intimacy and sexual desire, so you're in the right place!

Even though you no longer have the help of chemicals and hormones, which once made flirty behavior happen so naturally, you can still enjoy romantic and flirtatious interactions with your partner. Do you think this is possible? We'll put this theory to the test at the end of the chapter.

Tap into Technology

I don't know what generation you're from, but I'm from Gen X—the cross-over generation from pre-technology to the age of technology. These two eras are worlds apart in the way we communicate, including both normal and flirty exchanges.

If you're from my generation, do you remember your old rotary dial house phone with the long, I mean, *really long* cord? To dial someone long distance would take a full 30 seconds, and God forbid you misdialed and had to start all over again. Or if the line was busy! (Busy signals...now that's funny.) Have you ever called someone in anger with a rotary dial phone? How you would jam your finger in the hole and whip it around as fast and hard as you could and then wait impatiently for it to come back to the starting position, to whip the next number around? Or did you ever hide in a closet for a private conversation, only for your mother to track you down because the trail of phone cord gave your location away?

Please forgive me! I'm having a moment of nostalgia here.

By the way, if you don't know what I'm talking about, go to your great grandma's house if she's still plugging along and give her rotary phone a try. It's a hoot!

Well, times sure have changed in drastic ways because of the world of technology we live in today, haven't they? Lucky you, it's easier than ever to take advantage of fun ways to flirt with your partner. I can't imagine you haven't, but you never know. Flirting through technology can be very stimulating and make a long day go by quicker when you carve out some playtime with your man. Have you taken selfies for him, naked or otherwise? Or have you sent him a picture of you bent over in his favorite underwear? Do you flirt just to arouse him, or tease him about all the naughty things you will do when he gets home? How about a little video peepshow when you're in the ladies' room at work? Do you ever send him a text to let him know how horny you are? Have you ever given him a FaceTime masturbation show?

Maybe it sounds like I'm speaking a foreign language to you, but these are examples of easy yet important sex-related activities necessary to keep the spirit of fun alive. These flirty activities help build feelings of excitement and anticipation leading to the act of sex itself.

Do you know how many men and women in monogamous relationships do what I'm describing, but not with their respective partners? I honestly don't know how many people partake in this type of activity; however, I'm certain it's way more than it should be (which should be none). Both men and women who find excitement outside their relationships work themselves into a frenzy because it's something fresh and thrilling. But the truth is, anyone can have the same kind of excitement with their long-term partner, and it can be equally as exciting.

Angel and I have been together for many years, and we're proof-positive it's possible to enjoy each other now as much as we did at the beginning of our relationship. Because we share the same desire to keep our flame of passion and excitement burning, we're on a never-ending quest to maintain a spicy sex life.

I'll share with you just one example of how we keep our relationship fresh and filled with sexual intimacy using technology. Although we've gotten each other sexually worked-up countless times, not that long ago we got into such a frenzy of sexual anticipation that when we finally had sex, it was *through-the-roof* passionate!

On a laid-back Saturday morning, I was relaxing outside on our back porch and he was awake in bed. I sent him a few flirty texts, and naturally, he responded. And so began our *dance of seduction*. As our flirtatious texts flew back and forth, the conversation became more and more heated, filled with loads of suggestive language and graphic details about what we were going to do to each other. The buildup of sexual energy was so hot and exciting that when he finally told me to come to the bedroom, I opened the door to find my very excited husband ready to enact all the dirty talk we had just exchanged. I pounced on that man like a wild animal attacking its prey. We ravaged each other with such passion and desire like two crazy, sex-starved strangers, not like a married couple who had already been together for over a decade.

Long-term relationships can become flat-out dull if you allow juicy flirtation to dry up. It's another aspect that requires effort, but that doesn't mean you should kiss it goodbye. It just means you must work hard to keep it alive!

Many couples participate in flirty and seductive behavior that makes them feel amazing at the beginning of their relationship, but they mistakenly let it slip away. If this type of behavior has faded into the past, you must work hard to reintroduce it now and continue to maintain it into the future. Once you've reintroduced flirty and seductive behavior, you will progress to the next phase of relationship rebuilding, which coincidentally is the next chapter!

Honest Assessment

1. Do you still flirt with your man in any way? If not, why not?

YES / SOMETIMES / NO

2. Does he still flirt with you? If so, how do you respond? Are you playful, do you ignore him, or do you become annoyed?

YES / SOMETIMES / NO

3. Have you ever sent him suggestive, flirty text messages, or naughty pictures of yourself? If so, how often? If not, why not?

YES / SOMETIMES / NO

4. What specific efforts do you put into being flirtatious with your man?

____

____

____

5. Do you compliment his appearance, like his sexiness or manliness?

YES / SOMETIMES / NO

6. Do you still make sexual innuendos or approach him with suggestive body language?

YES / SOMETIMES / NO

7. Do you express to him by text, phone, or in-person how you can't wait to be with him sexually?

YES / SOMETIMES / NO

Sexercise: Sexting + Hot Date = Passionate Sex

Through flirty and suggestive sexting, your mission will be to create a buildup of sexual energy and anticipation for a hot date and passionate sex by the end of the week. Make any necessary plans prior to this Sexercise to execute your date flawlessly by the weekend.

At the beginning of the week, replace your typical all-business text bullets such as **pick-up milk on the way home** or **I'm taking the girls to their dance lesson now**, with more lighthearted, flirty messages that allow him to reply in the same way. Ask him how his day is going, tell him you're thinking of him, or that you can't wait to see him later. You will gradually build to sexting by mid-week, but keep these initial exchanges light and sweet. You don't want to send him a picture of you spread-eagle on Monday and text *Meet me Friday at The Tipsy Cow at 9 pm sharp* with no buildup. Well, you could do that, but you might utterly confuse him.

If he doesn't engage right away with your flirty efforts, don't give up. Give him a minute... he'll catch on. By the end of Tuesday, send him a picture of you wearing something sexy and looking seductive. On Wednesday, text him an invitation to meet up for a drink. Assuming he says yes, emphasize how much you can't wait to hang out.

Alright, you're at the point where you're creating the sexual buildup for your date. Playfully tease him with small details and excited anticipation about how awesome it will be to spend alone time outside of the house. Describe the sexy wear you'll have on under your clothes or that you'll be bra- and pantie-free. By Thursday and Friday, you should be explicitly detailing your sexual agenda and feel a rush of excitement every time you describe to him your desires for the evening. Continue sexting suggestive and downright naughty innuendos, right up to your date night.

This date night would be a great opportunity to wear what you bought back in Key Three: Confidence!

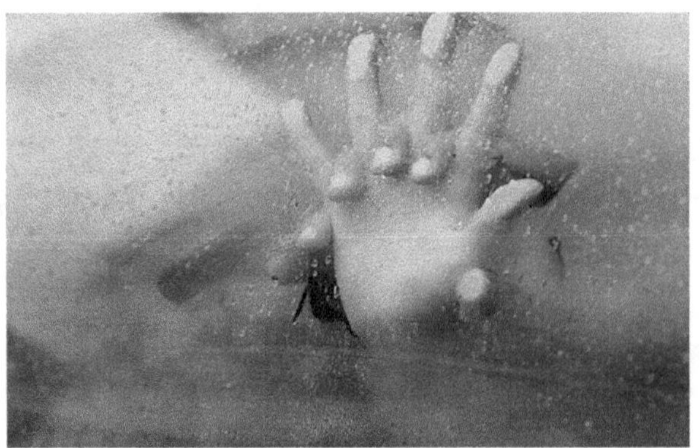

The goal of this Sexercise is to coax your little sex vixen to come out and play like she used to. Enjoy this carefree and exciting *dance of seduction* with your partner again. As I've already said, I don't care how long you've been together, you're both still capable of getting excited from playful flirtation. The best part is that you've known him forever, the advantage being you can say or do whatever you want to get him worked up, without limitations!

Before I go into the details of your date, just a heads-up to keep the alcohol consumption in check on this enjoyable evening together. Stick to no more than two drinks so you're both coherent. There's nothing wrong with a little buzz, but you shouldn't be three sheets to the wind. You will take separate ride services to meet up but share one for your ride home. When you get to your house, don't go inside. Go straight to the back seat of your parked car. You're now at the point of engaging in a passionate sexual encounter created by a week-long buildup of flirting, teasing, and spending a fun and relaxed night out together.

Tease your man with your sex appeal and seduce him. Make moves that aren't part of your normal routine. Be sensual and act like the boss. Passionately kiss his neck, unbutton his shirt, kiss his chest, and tease his nipples with your tongue. Unbutton his pants and rub his penis on the outside of his underwear. By now, you should both be bursting with overwhelming excitement and frantically trying to rip each other's clothes off to have sex.

If you follow this outline, I feel confident you will enjoy yourselves immensely and have passionate sex like you haven't had in a long time. You'll wonder why you haven't taken the time to enjoy yourselves like this for so long. And hey, this activity doesn't have to be one and done. If you both really enjoyed this Sexercise, whose stopping you from making it a weekly, bi-monthly, or monthly outing? This journey is all about bringing excitement and sexual intimacy back to your relationship. Continue to reconnect with each other in ways you will both enjoy...*and keep it going!*

My SIM Journal

List at least five ways you were flirtatious and seductive with each other during the Bliss Zone of your relationship. Reincorporate these same activities now and as you move forward. Also, after you've completed the Sexercise in this chapter, write about your experience and the feelings that accompanied your week filled with flirting, your hot date, and passionate sex. Did this experience create a renewed sense of excitement for each other? If not, write down why you believe the sparks weren't flying, and try this Sexercise another time after you've discussed what you can do differently that may work better.

The Key to the Dance of Seduction

The key to the dance of seduction is having the desire to bring your seductive abilities out of hibernation. To execute playful exchanges of flirtatious behavior, you must make the conscious decision to revive this part of your relationship. Only then can you begin the dance of seduction by flirting, teasing, and suggestively playing with your partner. Once you have reintroduced this sexy dance, the passion factor will naturally follow. Lucky you, that just so happens to be the next chapter.

KEY SEVEN
The Passion Factor

Do you know exactly *why* you're striving to increase flirtatious behavior with your partner so much? Well, it's to help rebuild passionate feelings for him! Passion is the factor that allows couples to enjoy an ongoing awesome sex life, no matter how many years they have been together. If you let passion slip away, it becomes yet another important connection that goes down with the ship and into the murky waters of less adoration, less affection, less intimacy, less communication, less... less...less.

Do you think it's possible for sexual intimacy with your partner to go from routine and mundane to juicy and passionate? I certainly do! That's why we're going to concentrate our efforts on passion for this next building block. Passion is the fuel that *creates* sexual desire. If your sexual relationship is in a serious drought, don't think for one second you're both not capable of bringing the passion back. It comes down to two factors: openness and willingness. You must possess the desire to please each other, coupled with an open mind to explore new sexual avenues. You have to break away from your current sex routine and actively seek new sexual activities you both find interesting, arousing, and stimulating.

Are you thinking that sounds impossible because you have felt nothing in the passion department for so long? And even worse, if his performance is yawn-provoking during sexual interactions, you may feel there's no real incentive to spend your energy on trying anything different. What if he can't even level up his game?

Remember, my mission is to help *you* revitalize the bond of sexual intimacy with your partner. Meaning, I'm here to offer *you* advice to improve this area of your relationship. So, here are some ideas to help remedy a passionless sex life and bring *the passion factor* back into the game.

Take the Lead

For starters, if you're in the middle of blah sex, decide to gently lead him to better enjoy your time together. If he's down between your legs doing a poor job giving you oral, don't give him the tap on the shoulder as if to say, *It's okay honey, you can come up now...you tried.* That's terrible for both of you. *Instead, use it as a teachable moment!* Explain what feels good to you. If he hits a spot that makes you feel pleasure, even if it's by accident because he's all over the place down there, take that moment to say, "Ah yeah, do that again, baby...like you just did...that feels so good." Or keep it simple and say, "Now go slow," or "Yes, right there."

Don't forego this pleasurable act just because you find it, ummm...*underwhelming* (bless his heart for trying). This scenario would actually be a great opportunity for a post-sex talk. Tell him how much you'd enjoy watching or reading something with a juicy oral sex scene before the next time you're together. After you're done watching/reading, tell him how aroused you felt during a particular scene. Encourage him to emulate what you watched/read that stimulated you so much. Be supportive and encourage him. Explain in a sexy way how much you would enjoy oral sex, just like what you saw/read.

Be Vocal

What if you were trying your absolute best to give him an expert BJ and he didn't make a peep? Not one word of positive reinforcement, or one pleasurable groan or grunt. He just stood, kneeled, or lay there quiet and lifeless, no response. How would you feel? Probably inadequate or insecure you weren't doing a good job because of the lack of verbal feedback.

When you express sounds of pleasure anytime during a sexual encounter, those sounds serve as a gauge of just how much pleasure you're experiencing. It's a compliment and serves as a reinforcement of a job well done. When you moan and groan, these sounds can stimulate your partner's excitement as well. The more sounds you make, the more excited he will become. I know when my husband says sexy and naughty things and moans and groans, it stimulates me to another level. I respond and engage in the same way, which creates a heightened passionate exchange with each other.

Now, I must mention, it's important not to be fake, super loud, or make exaggerated sounds like a porn star. You don't want to sound superficial. That's annoying to most men because they know it's not authentic and can inadvertently make them feel inadequate. Be natural with the sounds you make. You don't have to be loud—you only need to be audible enough so he can hear you.

If you make noises or tell him how good he's making you feel, he'll probably join you by saying some sexually stimulating words in return. Sexual noises and comments convey your level of enjoyment and can be very stimulating for both people.

Dress for the Occasion

Are you naked every time you have sex? Or do you wear the same nighty every time? No, no, no! *Always* wear something different for your sexual encounters. I assume you don't wear the same clothes to work every day. And why is that? Well, people would talk about you for one, but really, it's because you want to change your appearance and look good in a different way, every day. The same principle applies to your sex-time wear. Most men enjoy any type of sexual variety. Since your man is in a monogamous relationship with you, he can't experience sexual variety in the way of being with other women, so make it a point to change your wardrobe for him while on the bed.

Here are some sexy-wear ideas to switch things up:

- Sheer or lacy lingerie
- Just panties and topless
- One of his tees or dress shirts
- Nothing
- Short-shorts and a sports bra
- A silk nighty or robe
- A cotton strappy tee and boy shorts
- A thong and bra (or thong only/bra only)
- A sexy and form-fitting dress
- A work skirt or dress
- Roleplay attire

You get it...change up the visual for him! I feel confident he'll appreciate your efforts. Visit my store **www.simtoyshop.com** if you need some hot, new sexy wear. You will find a great variety of all things sexy to choose from to get you both excited!

Think Outside the Box

Have you ever considered incorporating sex toys, roleplay, sex in unconventional places, or even unconventional sex? If not, hang tight...Key Nine is right around the corner! Routine sex is synonymous with ***BORING*** sex. In a long-term relationship, you *must* be creative and introduce new sexual intimacy ideas, often. When you set your intention and devise well-thought-out plans to expand your sexual horizons, these actions invariably revitalize the passion factor. Continue perusing the SIM Toy Shop for roleplay outfits, sex toys, erotica, or just look around to see what items make you feel aroused when you think about adding them to your sexual goody box.

Make a Plan

Another factor that can make a difference between a normal sexual interaction and a *sparks-flying* sexual interaction is to plan "session time." Intentionally set time aside so you don't have to feel there's a race against the clock. You don't have to mark a day and time on a calendar a week in advance for your time together, but you can make a simple verbal agreement. For example, in the afternoon, plan to get together later that evening. Or maybe on a Wednesday, plan something for the weekend like a date night or role play to get excited about.

Planning allows the opportunity to create sexual anticipation so when you get together, you're already feeling excited about being intimate with each other, like the Sexercise you enjoyed in the last chapter. Although it's wonderful and exciting to be spontaneous, if short-term planning doesn't happen, a sexual interaction can otherwise feel rushed and other feelings can creep in and take over, like feeling too tired or too busy.

Kiss, Kiss, and Kiss Some More

If I could offer only one piece of advice to help bring passion back into your sex life, it would be this one. **Kissing is the gateway that leads to hot, passionate sex.** I'm not sure it's even *possible* to have passionate sex without lots of kissing.

If you no longer kiss before or during sex, this **100 percent, non-negotiable** must be reintroduced. Such a strong buildup of anticipation can happen during a make-out session, which in theory, should lead to passionate sex.

Sex without kissing is like a champagne glass filled with water. Yes, the water satisfies your thirst, but doesn't a glass of delicious, bubbly champagne sound a lot tastier? Kissing is an extremely important component to *the passion factor.* Focus on adding this steamy act of love back into your sex life. You will be amazed how this simple, yet effective element can create excitement. You will realize that kissing was that "missing something" in your sexual intimacy.

At the beginning of this guide, I explained how the bond of sexual intimacy plays a role in the ultimate success (or failure) of a relationship. Have you reflected on your current or past relationships while reading this guide? Does this statement hold truth for you, as it has for me?

I will share the difference sexual intimacy and passion, or lack thereof, has made in two of my relationships. In my last relationship, we allowed the bond of sexual intimacy to become buried under *life happening.* Neither my partner nor I did anything to remedy the situation. In my current relationship, we have worked hard to maintain sexual intimacy and passion through endless communication and a shared desire to nurture this part of our relationship.

The reason I share these two different experiences is not to compare these men as individuals.

The purpose is to show you exactly what can happen if you are or ***are not*** paying attention to the bond of sexual intimacy.

My intention is not to be disrespectful to my late husband by sharing this part of our relationship, but I would not be fully transparent if I didn't disclose our intimacy issues, which over time, became a big issue between us. It was a part of my life, our relationship, and partially what this guide is about—sharing relatable experiences so you don't have to feel alone with struggles you may be going through in your relationship.

* * *

John and I spent ten years together before he passed away. As with most other couples, the sparks flew between us for the first two years. After this period, our relationship moved from the Bliss Zone and settled into the Comfort Zone. We experienced many changes as a couple during our relationship. We moved far away from our families and built a successful business together. In the meantime, we brought two children into the world, became parents, and created our little family.

Since we were so far away from family and friends, it was us against the world. We juggled a plethora of responsibilities, all without a support system. Our daily grind was business and kids, kids and business. It was so rewarding, but so very exhausting. At the end of a long day handling business responsibilities, and the full-time duty of caring for two little boys until bedtime, there was nothing left to give by the day's end. Because our daily schedule was so busy, we crashed into bed with only sleep on our minds. Did I mention we had a family bed? Yes, we did.

Year after year, our sexual interactions became more infrequent, and passion was a mere memory of the past. Our relationship transformed primarily into business and child-rearing partners. It *seemed* acceptable that our sex life had been placed on the back burner, but it was a subject we never spoke about. It was more of an assumption because it was simply an unintended result of our busy lives. But as with many assumptions, it was wrong. As the bond of sexual intimacy steadily deteriorated, this missing piece began to fester. I thought he didn't care this bond had fallen to the wayside, because he never articulated his feelings about our virtually non-existent sex life. I thought he just felt like I did—absolutely exhausted at the end of a long day with no energy left for anything, including sex.

The frustration from this unaddressed issue slowly crept into other areas of our relationship and became the elephant in the room. Unfortunately, neither of us knew how to approach the problem, which affected our entire relationship. At the time, because I was in the middle of the situation, I couldn't see what a detriment this was to our relationship as a whole. I truly didn't understand the gravity of allowing our bond of sexual intimacy to slip away. However, I can now see so clearly the unintentional but ENORMOUS mistake we made.

Sadly, we never had the opportunity to turn this part of our relationship around before he passed away. It's hard to say how things would've panned out because we ran out of time. Although, I have to say, I'm not entirely convinced we would've been able to pinpoint the connection to other mounting problems stemming from this forgotten bond that got buried under the grind of life.

Let my experience serve as a realization or wake-up call for your relationship. If you genuinely still love your partner, show him in every way you love him, care for him, and want to be with him. Really *try* to enjoy every aspect of your relationship because frankly, it's emotionally draining to be with a person when it only evokes feelings of emptiness, discontent, or unhappiness within you.

And remember...*no one is promised tomorrow.* Most people live in the illusion they have infinite time to get things right, but that's simply not true. Make every moment and experience count in your relationship and life, so you never have to live with regretful thoughts of *coulda...shoulda...woulda.*

* * *

On the other end of the spectrum, Angel and I intentionally strive to keep the bond of sexual intimacy and passion going strong in our relationship. Although John and I carried a heavy load of responsibilities that do not challenge us, we still have our own basket of life's goodies to deal with. Just raising my teenage sons, at times, has felt like being swept into a vortex of insurmountable challenges accompanied by inconceivable levels of stress. I could not have imagined in my wildest dreams the rollercoaster ride of parenting, but that's a whole different topic for another book – ***Surviving Parenthood Without Completely Losing My Shit or The Shit Show of Parenting.*** I'm still undecided on the title, but either one is perfectly fitting.

Anyways, I believe the difference between my two relationships concerning the bond of sexual intimacy boils down to these two factors: choice and maturity. Angel and I have chosen to maintain this bond because we fully understand how critically important it is to an overall healthy relationship. I think John and I weren't mature enough to realize how important this bond was to maintain, or how solidly it connects to all aspects of a relationship. Sometimes we learn life lessons the hard way, and only in future situations are we given the opportunity to do things differently and get it right.

Here are some important factors I attribute to our strong bond of sexual intimacy and ongoing passion that keeps our sex life feeling fresh and new. First, we maintain a constant dialog through sexual communication. Second, acts of affection are a part of our daily interactions. Third, we both share a strong desire to please not only each other but ourselves. Fourth, we flirt with each other whether in person or through texts/pictures, and lastly, we're both very open-minded to try new and exciting ways to make our sex life interesting. Pretty much everything I've discussed so far in this guide helps keep our relationship fresh—there's a whole combination at play, which is exactly what I'm attempting to help you create in your relationship. We are solid proof that if you focus on keeping *the passion factor* alive (or reawaken it if it's gone to sleep), the sexual intensity between two people who've been together a long time can sustain itself.

However, if you let your sexual interactions decline into routine (AKA boring) sex, if you stop flirting and no longer show affection, you *will* not, you *cannot* have a hot and juicy sex life. It's impossible. So, work hard on *the passion factor* in your relationship. You must have this especially important piece of the puzzle to bring life not only back into your bedroom, but back into your whole relationship.

Honest Assessment

1. Do you feel there's any level of *the passion factor* in your relationship? Rate it from 1 to 10.

2. If your rating is below 5, for how long would you say it's been at this level?

3. If you rated your passion level 5 or higher, what factors do you contribute to maintaining this level?

4. Do you make sexual comments or noises while you're having sex to let him know you're feeling good? Does he?

You: YES / SOMETIMES / NO

Him: YES / SOMETIMES / NO

5. Do you ever guide him and tell him how to please you sexually? Does he ever guide you? Do either of you take offense or are you receptive to each other's suggestions?

You: YES / SOMETIMES / NO

Him: YES / SOMETIMES / NO

6. When you are having sex, what type of signals are you sending him? That you're enjoying or despising the action? Or that you're engaged or disconnected from the act? How does he respond to your signals?

____

____

____

7. When was the last time you two had passionate sex? Think back to that time. What made the experience feel passionate?

____

____

____

Sexercise: Turn Up The Passion!

This Sexercise will help reintroduce *the passion factor* back into your sex life.

Offer him a nice, sensual massage sometime this week. Who doesn't enjoy a good rub down? Tell him after his nighttime shower you have a little surprise for him.

When he comes out of the shower, have the bedroom ready with candles, music, and whatever you think will make him feel relaxed. Tell him to lay face down on the bed.

Treat your man to a sensuous massage with oil or lotion. When you're ready, tell him to flip onto his back. Start at his feet, move up his calves, thighs, and his inner thighs, but don't touch anything that may be standing at attention! Move to his arms and chest, then have a five-minute straight make-out session while you're on top of him. Really get into kissing. I mean *REALLY get into kissing!* Then work your way back down from his neck, chest, and stomach. Go to town however you wish once you're finally where he wants you, just make sure your man gets a happy ending, okay?

Did you know that giving your man a BJ makes him feel like he's **KING OF THE WORLD?** Let your man feel like he *is* a king, if only for a few minutes, will you? And you don't have to be the queen of deep throat, you honestly don't. Even if you suck and lick on just the head of his penis for a few minutes and stroke his shaft with one hand (or both if you're a lucky girl), trust me, he will be one happy and satisfied man. Another version of a highly enjoyable BJ is hands-free, so I'm told. You're only using your mouth and tongue, and while that can be a little tricky on your end, evidently it feels awesome for the man. Give it a try and get his feedback in your post-sex talk.

If you'd like to take this Sexercise a step further or use this idea another time, you can give him a BJ while he's asleep. One night, sneak under the sheets and start slowly and gently at first so he's still sleeping when he becomes aroused. You can go to town after he wakes up. It would be any man's dream to be woken by his woman between his legs pleasuring him. **I am 100 percent assured this is a no-fail mission!**

My SIM Journal

Write about the beginning of your relationship and what fueled *the passion factor*. Did you enjoy hot sex after a fun-filled date night? Did you create a buildup of excitement through sexting and then ravage each other? Did you kiss endlessly and focus on your partner's pleasure? What made you *want* to have sex? What parts of this type of excitement do you miss the most? This journal entry is meant to jolt your memory so you can incorporate those elements back into your relationship starting *today*.

The Key to the Passion Factor

The key to reintroducing *the passion factor* back into your relationship is first to master the dance of seduction. Once playful and flirtatious behavior has been rekindled, this opens the door for passion to come back into play. Actively find ways to make yourself feel sexy and think outside the box for new ways to experience sexual encounters. And remember, you can't enjoy the highest level of passion without kissing and then kissing some more! So put some chapstick on and pucker up!

KEY EIGHT
Power of the Mind ... Magic of the Moment

It's another Friday night. The week is *finally* over. Yay! You reward yourself with two, maybe even three, celebratory glasses of wine for making it through another long and crazy week. You're loosening up and feeling slightly tipsy, which once in a great while makes you feel a little amorous. You easily coax your man upstairs to the bedroom and take your clothes off, haphazardly tossing them onto the floor. Once you get on the bed, you treat him to a reverse cowgirl ride because you know that's his top favorite position and tonight, you want to please him.

You're riding along *(Yeehaw!)* and *oh snap,* here it comes...

Dammit, you think, *I have to get the oil changed in the car tomorrow, but it'll have to wait until after soccer practice.... Why does the soccer coach have practice at 8 o'clock on Saturday morning, anyway? Doesn't he have a life? ...Oh yeah, I can't forget to take the steaks out of the freezer tomorrow morning for dinner tomorrow night.... I don't know why my in-laws have to come over so often to eat. Don't I have enough on my plate without having to entertain them? I wish we didn't live so close, but then again, it does come in handy when we need them to watch the kids....*

All the while, you're riding away not skipping a beat, or should I say, pump. Has this scenario happened to you? It's okay, you can admit it. I told you I was non-judgmental! It's probably happened to you once, twice, or a thousand times. If you allow your mind to wander during sex, not only will it wander, but it may also end up fleeing the scene! It happens to **ALL** of us. Does the "wandering mind syndrome" happen to you more often than not during sex? Or worse, are you wishing for sex to be over before you even get started? If so, we'll be working on realigning your mind and body so they can synchronize with each other again. When a couple is together for a long time, it can be challenging to stay focused during sex, *especially* routine sex. To remedy this issue, you will have to change your thought process to help your mind engage in the physical action. Is this possible? You know by now that I believe it is!

It is suggested we have approximately 60,000 to 70,000 thoughts bombarding our minds every day. Most of these thoughts come from either reliving the past (memory) or worrying about the future (imagination). Because our mind is anywhere but *here and now* much of the time, it's difficult for most people to experience the present moment. Yes, we all experience every minute of every day *physically* present wherever we are. But often, we are mentally far, far away from whatever activities our bodies are involved in...for example, sex.

This implies our inner world robs us from experiencing life to its fullest. Though I'm sure we were designed with this seemingly flawed aspect of the human experience with purpose, it's a challenge most people will not be able to conquer.

Why does the mind constantly expend so much energy on memory and imagination, when we can only truly experience the essence of life in the moment happening, well...*right in the moment?* Life can be enjoyed to the fullest when our mind and body align with each other. Few people pay attention to this, and so, most people miss the countless, amazing opportunities to experience life in beautiful and enriching ways.

Do you ever take a moment to "smell the roses" as the old saying goes? We all experience little tastes of what it means to be present; however, most people don't linger in the moment as much as they should. (It should be most of the time, by the way.) Do you ever stop, I mean completely STOP whatever you are doing, and without any distractions appreciate a beautiful sunset unfold into a spectacular array of shapes and colors? Or enjoy the sensation of a warm ocean breeze touching your face, or closely watch in wonder as a butterfly flutters amidst flowers? When is the last time you enjoyed a baby's laughter, or were completely immersed in a great book? Were you fully engaged while someone spoke to you, instead of thinking about your grocery list? This is it. These seemingly insignificant moments may seem trivial, but they hold immense importance to being present and the gifts it offers. If there's a willingness and desire to connect to the experience, it's always right there to enjoy.

So then, doesn't it stand to reason that being fully present during sexual intimacy is an amazing gift of life as well? Yes, I believe it *is* a gift. Humans were created for our bodies to come together as one, and certain feelings and sensations can only be experienced by this union. We should focus on every touch, every move, and every sensation during moments of intimacy we share with our partner—never dreading the interaction or wishing for it to end.

When you're in the middle of sex and your mind meanders away, how can you possibly expect to feel excited and passionate when it's your **mind** that creates sexual pleasure? It's not your body *creating* it; your body is simply *responding* to your mind's lead. Therefore, if your mind is **completely focused** on the physical activity, you're bound to have an amazing sexual experience, or at minimum, a good time. In the same way, if your mind travels to Planet X while you're having sex, you probably won't experience much enjoyment, if any at all. You might even wish it were over so you can do more important things, like take out the garbage. I want you to understand on the deepest level how strongly your body is connected to your mind, so let's look at a few examples.

If you have a thought that evokes fear, your heart might start pounding. Maybe you begin to sweat, and your body tenses and goes into fight-or-flight mode. How about when you feel sad? How does your body respond? You might feel a heaviness or aching in your heart. You probably cry, and your digestive system responds by either losing your appetite or feeling the need to overeat. Now, think about how happy you feel when you daydream about that awesome vacation you just finished planning. Every time you visualize yourself on that tropical island sipping mojitos and listening to Caribbean rhythms, or gazing into the vast ocean from the cruise ship deck with your flowing dress dancing in the wind, or walking around Disneyland having an absolute blast with your family...don't these thoughts make you feel giddy with excitement? Doesn't your heart flutter and feel like bursting from pure happiness? The anticipation of the trip surges through your body and you feel great. You're experiencing emotions and physical responses solely through your thoughts.

Your body reacts to thoughts about sex in the same ways. For example, if your thought process is one of impatience or annoyance during sex, like, *Ugh, when is this Neanderthal going to finish up and get off me?* Or *It's been five whole minutes already–I want to go to bed...what's his hold up?* Do you *honestly* think you will enjoy yourself on any level? And what kind of vibe do you think these thoughts send him? That you're enraptured in the moment and thoroughly enjoying yourself? Doubtfully *that* vibe. Or that you'd rather be doing *anything* else other than having sex with him? Yeah, probably *this* vibe. Now on the flip side, what if you were thinking hot and sexy thoughts like, *Damn, this feels so good, I don't want it to end, or, I can't believe how amazing sex is after all these years. He's such a good lover; I love having sex with him.* In this case, you will not only enjoy yourself immensely, but you will also relay this information through your engaging physical responses, which creates an awesome cycle of goodness.

Think back to the beginning of your relationship. It was **effortless** to lose yourself in the moment of sexual intimacy, wasn't it? You were completely immersed mentally and physically when you were together. Your focus was directly on enjoying and savoring his gentle touch, his passionate kisses, and every sexual word he whispered in your ear. Keyword: FOCUS. Because you enjoyed being with him so much, your mind wanted to be nowhere else, and so it stayed put for the action.

If your sex life has slipped into a routine, which is often the case in a long-term relationship, your mind can feel like it's "off duty" because if you're only going through the motions, why is it needed anyway? Your mind would rather hash out more important things like what new color to paint your bedroom or how your new boss is such a pain in the ass with his nonsensical micro-management crap.

So, to *enjoy* the moment, you must be *in* the moment. There's really no other way, because your body and mind work hand-in-hand during sex. If your mind isn't present, your body will only go through the physical motions, making it seem like a chore more than anything else. Don't you have enough obligatory duties already? Don't make something as amazing as a good sexual connection with your partner humdrum. Washing dishes is humdrum. Waiting in a doctor's office is humdrum. Paying bills is humdrum. Sex should *not* be humdrum.

And Now ... *Drumroll Please* ... The Big O

There are many studies regarding the woman's ability to orgasm during sexual intercourse. After researching the most current data, I am unable to quote an exact percentage of how many women can and can't, because the stats differ based on each study. But the bottom line is that many women, while able to climax through oral play, finger stimulation, and sex toys, cannot climax through intercourse.

An orgasm is the most intense and pleasurable sensation a woman can experience. It's pure ecstasy, hands-down. Anyone who knows how to achieve an orgasm will tell you the same. What an amazing gift for women. I say ***women*** because the clitoris has about 8,000 nerve endings while our fellow friend Mr. Penis Head has only half that amount. So, if orgasming during intercourse has evaded you, it's positively worth it to figure out once and for all how to harness the power of this euphoric sensation during penetration!

Masturbation vs Penetrative Sex Orgasms

If you can achieve an orgasm through masturbation, there's a good chance you can also achieve one through sexual intercourse. But you must take your mental block off and open your mind. Do you want to hear something funny? I'm the opposite of most women. I shared with you back in Key 4: Self-Exploration how much I explored my body as a teenager. And I did. However, I never figured out how to bring myself to orgasm. For one, my pesky sister was always around, unknowingly blocking my attempts. And two, I was lucky enough to experience orgasms shortly after I began having sex, so I didn't feel the need to keep trying to achieve them on my own anymore.

This was very unfortunate because I was sexually inactive for about six months while in

between relationships. I nearly killed myself trying to have an orgasm through masturbation. My only chance was when I went to bed, hoping to have a wet dream. I was climbing the walls with frustration for those six long, non-orgasm-filled months.

I'm happy to say, after much tenacity and determination, I can finally bring myself to orgasm, but it's still a process for me using fingers alone. (And that's why I have my trusty vibrator...who needs the struggle?) If you know how to give yourself the ultimate pleasure, you're already halfway there! All you need to do is learn the correct positioning with your partner to have an even better orgasm. Yes, I said *better!*

I once read an article stating that a masturbation orgasm is better than an intercourse orgasm. Do you know what I have to say to that? *No way! Nah-uh! No-no-no!* Whoever wrote that article clearly never experienced an earth-shattering orgasm through intercourse. My personal experience has been that intercourse orgasm is more mind-blowing than a masturbation orgasm, and I don't say that just because I'm not an expert in the latter. For me, a masturbation orgasm feels what I would describe as more intense and concentrated just in that area of my body, while an intercourse orgasm creates a euphoric sensation throughout my whole body. I know there are many variables and every woman's body is different, but please don't wave your white flag if you may have heard incorrectly you weren't missing anything.

If you really think about it though, it makes sense why so many women can orgasm through masturbation rather than sexual intercourse with their partner. When a woman plays with herself, it's because she feels horny and wants to experience physical pleasure and a sexual release. Doubtfully her mind is wandering aimlessly, and her focus is on the action at hand.

On the contrary, when a woman has sex in a long-term relationship, there's probably only a 50/50 chance she's even interested in having sex. If she doesn't feel in the mood, her mind will be elsewhere, and she'll just go through the physical motions. What does this mean? I think it means that if her mind isn't present and she's not feeling any type of excitement, it will be virtually impossible for her to orgasm.

To make matters worse, it is (unfortunately) rare for a woman to have a partner who believes that sex is all about *her* pleasure. When the focus is revolved more around his pleasure, paired with the pressure to orgasm, this combination can create an even stronger mental block. It can be difficult for an orgasm to happen when there's any type of active mental block going on.

On an interesting side note, did you know that some women, no matter what, won't be able to achieve orgasm through intercourse? The distance of the clitoris and urinary opening needs to be 2.5 centimeters, or slightly less than one inch. This seems to be a huge factor in whether climax will occur through intercourse. Even during sex, most women who can orgasm do so through clitoral stimulation by rubbing, grinding, and friction created between the clitoris and the man's pelvis.

Orgasm (or lack thereof) Study

A study was conducted on women about why they thought they had difficulty achieving orgasm through intercourse. There were 11 categories identified during the original focus group and study development, including a 12th "other" category. Here are the (disheartening) results:

1. I am not interested in sex with my partner.
2. My partner does not seem interested in sex with me.
3. I do not enjoy sex with my partner.
4. My partner does not seem to enjoy sex with me.
5. I am not sufficiently aroused/stimulated during sex.
6. I am not adequately lubricated during sex.
7. I experience pain and/or irritation during sex.
8. We do not have enough time during sex.
9. I am uncomfortable or self-conscious about my body/appearance.
10. I feel medication or a medical condition interferes with having an orgasm.
11. I feel my stress and/or anxiety makes it difficult for me to have an orgasm.
12. Other.

The most common overall reasons given by women were stress and anxiety, reported by 58 percent; lack of enough arousal or stimulation by nearly 48 percent; and not enough time by 40 percent. Moderately common issues were negative body image, reported by 28 percent; pain or irritation during sex by 25 percent; insufficient lubrication by 24 percent; and medication-related problems by almost 17 percent. The "other" factors were less commonly reported by fewer than 10 percent of respondents.

Hmmm...

What I take from these responses are two main factors creating a huge disconnect. First, there seems to be a lack of sexual communication between couples, and second, the woman's perception of sexual intimacy with her partner. Did you notice that many reasons were not physical issues? They were mental issues blocking their ability to orgasm. Just saying...

The Mind: An Orgasm's Best Friend or Worst Enemy

Since we're on the topic, let's talk about how important of a role the mind plays in orgasming. I'll use my experience to explain just how powerful the mind's role is for a woman. I've never had a problem orgasming, and most of the time we're intimate, I do. (Well, aren't I fancy?) However, there are times during the act of sex that my mind wants to travel. No matter how skillful I am in moving my body to achieve an orgasm, it won't happen. Overall, I'm disciplined about staying in the sexual moment, but sometimes random or troubling thoughts *will* get the best of me. If my focus isn't on what I'm doing, like how I'm moving, how he's moving, and the sensations I'm feeling in my vagina, guess what? As orgasmic as I am, I won't be able to climax. If my mind is blocked by distracting thoughts, so is my orgasm. If I'm not connected to the act mentally, it simply won't happen. I believe the mind is by far the biggest contributing factor for women who can't orgasm during sex. As noted in the study, only 17% to 25% of women believe it's a physical issue blocking their ability to orgasm.

For the length of time I've been in my current relationship, I've been able to orgasm in almost every sexual position you can imagine. If beforehand someone told me this was possible, I would have insisted it was absolutely impossible. I knew how to orgasm in my one trusty position–on top. For over twenty years of sexual activity, this was all I knew. I was able to orgasm during intercourse, and that was good enough for me. However, the sexual openness Angel and I share, staying present while being intimate, and his desire to please me, has allowed my physical pleasure to expand, immensely.

This trifecta is extremely important to help achieve orgasms: great sexual communication, staying present during sex, and having a partner who has a sexual skill set along with *the desire to truly please you.* If your partner isn't trying his best to please you in the many ways a woman can experience pleasure, work together through sexual communication to change this. It takes more energy and willingness, but the result is worth the extra effort. Motivate him by explaining how much more enjoyable your sexual interactions can be if he tries pleasing you in ways you find exciting. For example, if you love oil massages on your vagina, or you become highly aroused when he pinches your nipples, or you get a thrill to dominate or be dominated, LET...HIM...KNOW!

No Faking! (If you're into that sort of thing.)

Are you aware that faking an orgasm is incredibly insulting to a man? Trust me on this one. He would rather you be honest about not being able to orgasm than insult his intelligence by trying to pull off a fake, mercy orgasm. If you fake orgasms, even though you may do it with good intentions, your slick little move non-verbally says one of two things to him. Either it says, "You can't make me feel good enough to have an actual orgasm, so let me fake one to feed your ego and make you feel better about yourself," or, "I just want this to be over with already, so let me pretend I had one, so we can wrap up this party."

Men can be very intuitive, and some men care enough to pay attention to the authenticity of a woman's orgasm. There's a good chance that if you fake orgasms, he knows, which can be a big blow to his ego. But even if you've pulled the wool over his eyes a thousand times and he doesn't have the beginning of a clue you're pretending, wouldn't it be better for both of you to experience *real* orgasms during sex? A female orgasm is also highly pleasurable for the man because he feels a sense of accomplishment when he knows he's given his woman the ultimate pleasure. Even though the male plays only a partial role, he may take your inability to orgasm personally.

Sometimes, if I have a mental block and I know I won't be able to orgasm, I give my husband a code phrase like "Go on without me" or "Don't worry about me." He appreciates my honesty, and he's very thankful I never try to fake an orgasm. If I can't, I can't. But I won't lie, I'm curious if he could tell if I faked an orgasm...just once. I wonder if I could pull one off!

In conclusion, if you fake orgasms...***stop!*** He more than likely doesn't appreciate the gesture. Forget about your best Meg Ryan impression from the movie *When Harry Met Sally*. Listed below are some techniques to help you achieve the Big O with your man, authentically.

Intercourse Orgasm Tips

- ✓ **Set your intention.** Try to have an orgasm the next time you're sexually intimate. Share your intention so you can plan together.
- ✓ **Create the mood.** When the time arrives, set the mood for yourself. Make whatever preparations necessary to help you get in the mood—music, candles, a glass of wine, a

couple hits of marijuana (if you're in a legalized state), complete darkness, erotica, adult videos, sex toys, or a combination of these ideas. It's important to prepare not only your environment but also your mental state for complete relaxation. The buildup is a big contributing factor leading to sexual excitement, which can help you achieve an orgasm.

- ✓ **Shut the world out.** Make sure you will not be rushed or disturbed. There's nothing worse than being interrupted during sex or feeling a sense of urgency like there's a stopwatch next to the bed. A good time would be right after you put the kids to bed, during their nap time on the weekend, or when they're at someone else's house.
- ✓ **Positioning.** In my personal experience, achieving an orgasm is still the easiest on top. It's the movement more than the position itself. Because you're orgasming through clitoral stimulation, you have to move your hips in a way that your clitoris is rubbing against his pubic area. If he props himself up a little with a few pillows, it will offer more contact. This isn't a bounce up and down action, it's a grinding move. Envision the movement like riding a mechanical bull. Once you get in a rhythm, you are the one controlling the speed of your movement. Place his hands on your waist and have him press down slightly to create a little more friction between your vagina and him. Rather than resting your lower legs on the outside of his thighs, bring them up and over so your feet are resting on the inside of his thighs. This offers more control and pressure in your pelvic region.
- ✓ **Focus.** Remove any floating thoughts other than orgasming. Imagine the climax building and place your thoughts entirely on what you feel in your vagina. Be patient. Communicate to him verbally if you need him to adjust his position or anything else. He won't be the one moving, so you're in control. Don't become frustrated if it doesn't happen, just try another time. The more you and your partner communicate about this and try different ways to bring you to orgasm through intercourse, the better. This mission alone will create sexual excitement because you're both striving for a common goal, which is to make you feel amazing.

Honest Assessment

1. Do you ever make genuine connections with the present moment? If so, how? And how often?

YES / SOMETIMES / NO

____

____

____

2. When you connect to the present moment, how does it make you feel inside? Are you aware of the connection when it happens?

____

____

____

3. When you're having sex with your partner, do you find yourself:

A. Completely immersed in the moment
B. Present most of the time, but your mind wanders occasionally
C. Half of the time present and half of the time thinking about non-related things
D. Your mind is somewhere else most of the time, only realizing sporadically that you're in the middle of having sex
E. Your mind is on a different planet...you don't know what the hell just happened

4. When you have sex, do you set the mood? Do you prepare your environment to make it feel special? Or is sex more like a business transaction?

____

____

____

5. How often do you want sex to be over? How much do you think about not enjoying what's happening?

---

6. Can you achieve orgasm either through masturbation or intercourse? If so, how often? If not, what's your opinion about why you can't?

---

7. Do orgasms completely evade you through both intercourse and masturbation? If so, have you tried researching techniques and suggestions online? Or have you tried sex toys?

Sexercise One: Write An Erotica Story

I want you to write your own erotica story. "Say what?" you say. "Yes!" I reply. This is one of your assignments in this chapter! I don't care if your writing skills aren't developed beyond scribbling a generic note at the bottom of a greeting card, or if you're a full-blown novelist. Tap into your inner Jackie Collins and write a sexy, lust-filled story filled with passion and excitement. I know you can do this!

Create your erotica around a sexual experience you had some time in your life that was *oh so* delicious, or maybe a fantasy you've always kept to yourself but would love to experience. It doesn't matter; it won't be read by anyone but you. However, if your man accidentally stumbles across it one day, you don't want him to find a hot and steamy story about you and another man (or woman, or both), so play it safe and use fictitious names. The story length doesn't matter either, just stay focused on the content.

Give yourself permission to feel a sense of freedom in this Sexercise. Let the thoughts flow from your mind through your hand and onto paper (use your journal), on your keyboard, or in your phone. Use your mind's eye when in creation-mode. Lots of visualization makes for a super-hot story. Your body's arousal while writing is a direct reflection of how much your mind is immersed in creating your story. The juicer, the better. Details, details, details! Let loose and be graphic. Use many descriptive adjectives. There's no such thing as over-describing in erotica!

This Sexercise should stimulate your mind enough to create arousal in your body. Your undies should be wet by the end of your story, or at a minimum, you should feel a tingle of excitement between your legs. Experience the physical reaction to your thoughts. It's a good practice to better understand the mind's effect on the body, especially about sensual thoughts.

Sexercise Two: Just Be There...

The next time you have sex, try being completely in the moment. I want you to just be there with him mentally and nowhere else in your mind. From beginning to end, keep your focus on what's happening in the moment and only in the moment. Undoubtedly, your mind will try to take off, but that's okay. Continually and gently coax it back to the present.

Start by setting the mood for yourself. Wait, wait...back up! Start by making sure you're alone in the house. Okay, now you can pull out the candles or dim the lights and tell Siri or Alexa to select your slow-jams playlist. You can't go wrong with some smooth R&B or Lo-fi chill beats playing in the background. Wear something sexy so you feel sexy. Let your man know you will be having a **session** so he can prepare by taking a shower, brushing his teeth, and maybe giving himself a spritz of cologne.

A "session" takes time, so if he's a minute man (and I really hope for your sake he's not), a whole session might be a stretch. If this is the case, you have a couple options. You can have a quickie or give him a BJ so he can ejaculate. Then, you can move onto your session after he has recovered. There are also endless ways to sexually stimulate each other through foreplay without involving the penis until the end. Don't get frustrated if he gets overly excited. After all, he won't know what the heck's going on and why you're so far off course from your normal sex routine. Chances are he will become overly excited and if he does, be patient and understanding.

During your session, guide him. Tell him what makes you feel good. Move his hands to where you want him to focus. Thoroughly enjoy the sensation of your body being touched. Focus on making and maintaining your mind/body connection. Close your eyes and think about the erotica you wrote.

A big part of the stimulation I experience during sex is created when my husband takes his time to make me feel pleasurable physical sensations. But an equally important element that adds to my excitement are visualization techniques I use. Whether he's exploring my body, giving me oral sex, or we're in the middle of the act itself, sometimes I close my eyes and imagine watching us like a voyeur. Other times, I imagine the pleasure he is experiencing from his perspective. Another great visualization technique I use is when we're in a position where I can't physically see penetration, I imagine being at a vantage point where I can. Visualizing him penetrating me combined with feeling the sensation of penetration gets me highly aroused.

Stay focused on the connection between your body and mind and I think you'll find your sexual experiences will be more enjoyable than they've been in a long time. If you create wonderful sexual experiences for yourself and your partner, your bond of sexual intimacy naturally will improve. As sex becomes new again, feelings of disinterest will fade and be replaced with feelings of excitement and anticipation between sessions.

My SIM Journal

For this journal entry write about your experience with Sexercise Two – *JUST BE THERE.* Note how you felt when you placed your full focus on being in the moment. Compare your typical sexual interactions to this one. Could you keep your mind from traveling? Did staying in the moment make you feel more aroused or engaged? If you didn't notice a huge difference, why do you suppose that is?

* * *

Don't give up if there wasn't a huge shift in your experience with this Sexercise. Every time you have sex, you know where your mind belongs. The more you practice, the more natural it becomes.

The Key to the Power of the Mind … Magic of the Moment

Create at least one intentional moment every day and be thoroughly immersed in it. This is a completely different experience of life, and it's just amazing. Wonderfully, you can experience this way of life every moment of every day. Get in the habit of keeping your mind and body in alignment, and you *will* experience life in a more beautiful and enriching way. Applying this same principle during moments of intimacy is the key to the power of the mind and to enjoying the magic of the moment.

KEY NINE
Fantasy Land

Now that you better understand the critical role your mind plays during sexual intimacy, let's head to the land of imagination and find out just how willing you are to take your sex life to the next level. Maybe you've already explored *Fantasy Land,* or perhaps you've only thought about it. Could it be this type of sexual exploration feels off-limits to you? Since you've made it this far through the guide, I believe you're open-minded enough to consider these fun ideas to help bring more excitement back into the physical aspect of your relationship.

Sex tends to become mundane when a couple has been together for many years. Mundane sex isn't exciting or passionate, is it? It's just...*meh.* If you're in this predicament, you probably already know the sequence of each position and how long the act itself will take before you even begin. There's no excitement involved, which is a vital ingredient to hot, exciting sex.

Now don your open-mind hat with boldness. We're going to explore some surefire ways to move away from ho-hum sex and over to *hot damn sex!*

Roleplay

Do you remember playing make-believe when you were a little girl? Maybe you dressed up like a princess, a magical fairy, or your favorite movie character. Wasn't it so much fun to step into the world of imagination? In that moment, you *were* a princess, a magical fairy, or your favorite movie character.

Now that you're a grown woman, who says you can't still have fun and play make-believe to escape reality every now and then? Even better, you can explore the world of imagination with your partner. Roleplay offers an opportunity to lose yourself in a different character far outside your normal personality, which to be honest, can feel quite liberating.

Roleplay also offers couples the chance to experience the freshness of being with a new partner, all the while staying within the boundaries of their relationship. I don't know about you, but this sounds like a win-win to me!

Are you concerned your acting skills won't win you a nomination for Best Actress? Don't be! We all know how to put on a different face and mold our character traits depending on what situation we're in, right? That's about the level of skill required for roleplay. And remember, as with anything new, practice makes perfect!

A great roleplay requires you to convince yourself that you're not *you* and he's not *him*. You know this isn't true, you just have to pretend it's true. This mind trick has nothing to do with wanting to be with another person. It's just a tool to stimulate the freshness that comes with a new sexual partner. Since you operate within the confines of a monogamous relationship, roleplay is a fun way to create this excitement. Read through the tips below so you'll have the confidence to execute an exciting and super-hot roleplay scenario.

ROLEPLAY TIPS

Character

For a successful roleplay, you must immerse yourself in your character and forget your normal identity. Because roleplay is acted with a fantasy character, "regular you" must leave the premises. (Sorry, *bye-bye!)*

Whatever character you choose, give her a different personality from your own, create a different look, carry yourself differently, and have a different attitude. If you're normally shy, be outgoing. If you're normally snippy or uptight, be nice and flirty. Alter your personality to fit the character you're playing. This is key to a successful roleplay.

If you want to play the role of an escort, tell your partner your name is Tiffany from Happy Ending Escort Service. You received a request to come to this address and take care of the man of the house. If you're Tiffany from Happy Ending Escort Service, then *dammit*...be her! You are not a housewife, you are not a businesswoman, and you are not a mom right now. At this moment, you are only Tiffany.

Be bold! Exude confidence and sexiness when you're in character. A big part of the fun is acting like someone completely different from yourself. Escaping life in this way feels carefree and refreshing!

Attire and Props

Make sure to purchase attire and props appropriate for your roleplay. These two elements are major players in making your fantasy character come to life. With some roleplay scenarios, you won't need anything special except your imagination. However, most roleplay scenarios will entail sexy roleplay attire. Check out **www.simtoyshop.com** for roleplay attire, props, and accessories.

Location

Don't limit yourself to your house. Many roleplays will happen there, yes. But don't exclude public places, your car, a hotel, or hooking up at a location you decide upon. I highly encourage roleplay outside your house because it takes this playful game to the next level. It also feels more believable and allows you to feel freer in your character. If you're playing the role of a naughty nurse or a sexy cleaning lady, for example, you can't very well play these scenarios outside your house. But if you're a call-girl, a stranger hook-up, or a newly single cougar out on your first date with a young stud, these are great scenarios to play in public.

Planning

If you're like every other ***Superwoman*** out there (because we ALL are), you're busy. *Very busy.* So, you must plan your roleplay. Make necessary arrangements for the kiddos if you have them. Think about what character you would love to pretend to be, such as a maid in your home, a stranger he meets at a bar for a casual hookup, or someone on a romantic first date. Buy the appropriate roleplay attire and make a mental game plan for your special night.

Decide if you're going to tell your partner about the roleplay you've chosen, so you can make a plan together, or do it with no warning, assuming he'll catch on. Either way is fun and exciting, and I suggest you play both ways.

Frequency

Make your goal to roleplay at least every eight weeks. You want enough time between each roleplay to build excitement, but not so often it resembles a routine. That said, if you both love to roleplay and find it drastically improves your sex life (which in theory it should), then play as often as you like! Plan scenarios both together and separately. Surprise each other occasionally. The anticipation and planning of roleplay is half the fun!

No Inhibitions

You might feel out of your element with this type of sex play, especially if you've never done it before. But honestly, don't knock it till you try it. I've had some of the most passionate, hot sex because of the anticipation and sheer excitement created through roleplay games. Roleplay is meant to be fun, engaging, and exciting for both of you. It's a chance to be uninhibited and to escape your normal routine, *especially* your sex routine.

A Must Mention

Some roleplay scenarios revolve around a scandalous affair or hooking up with a stranger—activities you wouldn't do in real life, *right?* Let there be no confusion here. **None** of these riskier scenarios means either of you want to cheat or be cheated on. It doesn't mean you want a new career as an escort or that you want to seduce the repairman. (If your repairman looks anything like mine, this would be the last roleplay you'd choose!)

Roleplay is a form of escapism, and typically, taboo situations create hot and thrilling scenarios. It's not reality nor is it a reflection of what you truly desire...it's just playful fantasy. Your imagination is the only limit to how much fun you can have with your roleplay adventures, so put your thinking cap on, because there are some awesome Sexercises coming up!

Fantasies

Now let's travel a little deeper into *Fantasy Land.* Yes, roleplay is in the family of fantasy, but it's more like a second cousin. You pretend to be a character and experience an exciting sexual encounter revolved around a chosen scenario. **Fantasies** are imagined sexual experiences that can play out in real-life situations...a whole different ball game.

Do you have any fantasies? Maybe you've imagined being ravaged by two men or a lesbian threesome with your man watching. Maybe you've fantasized about exhibitionist sex, voyeurism, or a Mandingo party, which is a combination of cuckolding and an orgy centered around one woman. The burning question is...*have you ever lived out a fantasy?* If so...lucky you! If not, like most of us who keep our secret fantasies locked away in our minds, there *is* an alternative way to experience your fantasies in your own bed and with your partner. I will reveal a unique technique in Sexercise Two that can create some amazing sexual experiences, but will require boldness on your part.

Until then, let's continue our journey through *Fantasy Land...*

Sex Toys

So come on, fess up...do you have a sex toy hidden somewhere in your bedroom? Or two? Or an arsenal of them like a man has 100 different weapons in his gun cabinet? Or are you a sex toy virgin? I personally have a treasure chest of them. Now, don't judge...I didn't say what *size* treasure chest!

For as long as I can remember, I've enjoyed using sex toys both solo and as a couple's activity. Well before the convenience of online shopping, I would occasionally visit a sex shop for a new toy. Sometimes I'd go alone and sometimes with my partner. I have to say, I found these shopping excursions very arousing because I was exploring new ways to experience sexual pleasure. I never felt embarrassed or ashamed to walk into a sex shop, surprisingly, since I did feel apprehensive about renting adult videos. But for some reason, those shopping excursions made me feel kind of daring and bold. I carried an "I don't care what anyone thinks" attitude. And guess what? Even though I now have my own online sex toy shop, once in a while, I'll still get in my car and drive to a sex shop to buy something, just for the thrill of the experience.

But I understand some people may feel reserved about this type of shopping trip. Nowadays, there's no need to walk into a sex shop if that's not your thing. Just hop online, type, browse, select, pay, and *voila!* An inconspicuous package is delivered to your doorstep in a few days. Easy-peasy.

There are so many options to explore in the vast world of sex toys. The selection is seemingly endless. My online store alone has thousands of items from roleplay and sexy attire to sex games, dildos, vibrators, luxury, and organic products. You name it, I probably carry it!

I created **www.simtoyshop.com** with the specific intention for women to feel they're in a safe and secure site while perusing sex toys. Even though there are a bazillion sex toy stores online, I have personally felt reluctant to make a purchase because many stores have an unprofessional feel, and I don't feel comfortable entering my credit card information. I figured, if I've felt this vibe, many other women probably have too.

It's important to me for women to feel at ease while shopping, so there are no viruses to fear, or annoying pop-up ads...it's just a simple and private browsing experience. Although my store is accessible through its direct domain name, it's also accessible within the confines of my website **www.sexualintimacymatters.com.**

Sex toy play is just one more great option to stir up some excitement! If you introduce (or reintroduce) this fun activity, your man is going to:

A. Think you've lost your mind, but in a good way.

B. Brag to his friends what a little sex vixen you're becoming again...he'll be so proud!

C. Wonder if this guide you're reading is creating all these new-found or revitalized sexual behaviors and ideas.

* * *

By now, you may be wondering how you're going to get yourself fully aroused to enjoy these sexual activities suggested in this chapter. Here's an idea to consider that's worked wonders for me.

Long before the birth of the internet *(ah-hem,* porn), I'd take a walk down to my neighborhood convenience store to buy an erotica magazine called *Penthouse Forum.* Maybe you've heard of it? It was a magazine where people submitted juicy sexcapades. Back then, I didn't know if they were real stories or a bunch of wannabe romance novel writers who had crossed over to the dark side, but at any rate...*my-my-my!* Talk about getting myself worked into a frenzy of sexual excitement!

To this day, I enjoy erotica because my mind taps into the story as I visualize the evocative scenarios unfold. I also write erotica, so whether I'm reading or writing, I become fully immersed in the whole experience. I think erotica is a great way to become aroused, especially if you're not into the visual stimulation of adult videos. In fact, many women prefer erotica over videos because the graphic narrative evokes sexual anticipation and excitement through imagination, which is often better than reality!

If you think reading erotica will tickle your fancy, here are some options to explore: Amazon carries countless juicy stories including every erotica genre you could possibly imagine. You might also find some good reads by doing an internet search for "erotica." Or go to **www.sexualintimacymatters.com/erotica** where you will find free stories to enjoy on my site.

In a long-term relationship, you absolutely must explore different ways to keep your sex life alive. When you combine your imagination with some props, you can create some amazing sexual experiences.

What's Your Position on Adult Entertainment?

Do you remember I told you there might be a topic or two that you may need to wear your open-mind hat? Even though you're already wearing it here in *Fantasy Land,* this might be one of those topics that pushes your comfort zone. Over the next several pages, I'll be discussing how society at large has become relatively desensitized to pornography and its prevalent use. I'll also discuss how this form of entertainment can have a positive or negative impact in a long-term relationship and share a story where a husband's use of pornography became a new hobby in the absence of sexual intimacy with his wife.

So, if you find the topic of adult entertainment offensive or off-putting and you would prefer to bypass this section, I completely respect that. Jump down to the HONEST ASSESSMENT questions. Otherwise, secure your hat and let's delve in...

Let's face it, adult entertainment, AKA pornography, has penetrated every orifice of technology. There's no denying its easy accessibility and solid presence in today's world of instant gratification. Since we're here in *Fantasy Land,* it's a great time to weigh in your opinion on the topic. For couples in long-term relationships, it can become a real nuisance and create unwanted problems, or it can be just another great tool to bring sparks back into the bedroom.

In a nutshell, adult videos offer the availability to watch any fantasy you've ever imagined be acted out by others. In the pre-internet era, if you wanted to watch adult videos, you had to drive to a video store, casually make your way to the back of the store, glance around to make sure no one saw you go behind the red curtain of shame with the sign that read **ADULTS ONLY,** and act nonchalant when setting your selected videos on the counter. Yes, I just dated myself, and yes, I rented adult videos from video stores as a young adult.

The point being, before the age of technology, it took a genuine effort and maybe some embarrassment or awkwardness to watch adult videos. The experience of accessing adult entertainment is incredibly different now. With just a couple of keystrokes, *BAM!* You've entered the world of sex, sex, and more sex.

Let's look at some statistics so you clearly understand the popularity of pornography in our modern world. Adult entertainment has become a multi-billion-dollar-a-year industry, with over 100 million internet users around the world visiting adult websites. One-quarter of search engine requests are sex-related, which equates to 68 million daily search engine requests. While women account for 28% of adult website visits, males account for 72% with the largest group being men between the ages of 35 and 49. *Wowzers!*

I think it's easy to understand the appeal of a private browsing experience (compared to the old days) and why the popularity of adult entertainment has skyrocketed. To me, it felt like there was a much stronger stigma attached to watching pornography before the internet. There was a seedy feel associated with it, so this pastime stayed mostly low-key because there was a fear of exposure or embarrassment. Because of its exceedingly easy access, I believe pornography has become more widely socially accepted. Younger generations are born into an age where this entertainment is literally right in their back pockets, so they don't have that taboo feeling connected to it like older generations. I'm told it's their "norm" and "no big deal." But just because pornography is used and accepted on a much broader spectrum nowadays, that's not to imply everyone is a proponent of this type of entertainment. In fact, it can become a great big problem in a relationship, especially if one partner opposes it.

Of course, there are all kinds of people who seek this form of entertainment for many different reasons, but I have a theory why so many men occupy themselves with this pastime. I believe it helps fill the intimacy gap with their partner. Think about it for a minute. We just learned the largest group of porn viewers are men between 35 and 49, and many men in that age bracket are in long-term relationships. Do you suppose that's a coincidence? I don't. Additionally, men experience a physiological buildup (never-ending sperm production), which can create a physical discomfort, as the term "blue balls" implies. If there's a lack of sexual activity in the relationship, guess what? That physical pressure needs to be released somehow. So, what's a man to do?

Maybe you agree, maybe not, but consider what I'm saying in an open-minded way. Say, for example, you and your partner have sex only a few times a month. Every day, a man can produce 70 to 150 million sperm or about 1,500 sperm per second. (Typical of the male species to go ***way*** beyond what is necessary to ensure the survival of humanity!) Now imagine the infrequency of sexual activity coupled with this ongoing *and excessive* sperm production. In the absence of a sexual release, some men will go to Plan B: a masturbation release. And many men who partake in Plan B will watch adult videos to help them reach orgasm. Based on this information, it seems like a feasible theory to me.

Here's a story that aligns with my belief of how easy pornography can fill the intimacy gap in a long-term relationship. Janie and Eddy are in their late 40s and have been married for 17 years.

* * *

Janie and Eddy sustained a strong bond of sexual intimacy well into the Comfort Zone years of their relationship. To keep things spicy, Janie often wore sexy lingerie, sometimes used sex toys, and occasionally watched adult videos as part of their foreplay. Eddy loved and appreciated the freshness of their sexual relationship and felt like a lucky dog when his friends would discuss their dried-up sex lives. Their sex life remained regularly active until Janie began perimenopause at age 45.

Slowly but surely, her interest in sex gradually lessened. By the time she turned 48, she reached full menopause, and her desire for intimacy had all but disappeared. Post-menopause sex turned into somewhat of an unpleasant experience for Janie. She felt pain and discomfort in certain positions. Her natural lubrication was replaced with store-bought, synthetic lube-in-a-tube, and her ability to easily achieve an orgasm turned into an arduous act. She frequently found excuses to evade intimacy because sex was now riddled with these new challenges that made it feel lacking and unfulfilling.

By the end of Janie's three-year transition, their sexual interactions had dwindled to around every two weeks, sometimes longer. This was a difficult adjustment for Eddy because they had been sexually active on average three times a week for years. He didn't know how to handle the situation because his sex drive was still the same, and his attraction and sexual desire for Janie were as strong as ever. He wanted their intimate relationship back to the way it was, but it was a moot point to discuss the issue because he understood her lack of interest wasn't her fault, or even her choice.

What to do...what to do?

To fill the void of infrequent sexual activity, Eddy decided the most viable solution would be to watch pornography to satisfy himself. At first, he felt conflicted because he only watched videos sometimes during foreplay with Janie. But since sex no longer included any type of foreplay, it seemed like a justifiable move. Initially, he felt guilty watching it on the sly. However, guilt quickly faded, and finding private moments for self-gratification sessions became a routine quest for Eddy.

Janie noticed Eddy was spending an unusual amount of time in his phone. Even when he was going to poop, he would take his phone and lock the door. Sure, he probably *was* pooping, but why did he have to lock the door? Janie was suspicious of these new behaviors and knew he was up to something, but exactly what, she didn't know. Had he met someone new at the office and they were sexting each other? Was he looking at dating apps? Janie inwardly acknowledged their sex life had changed drastically since she went through menopause, but she trusted him completely and never imagined he could cheat on her—he just wasn't the type.

One Saturday afternoon, Eddy was going to change the oil in his truck. On his way to the garage, he took his phone out of his pocket and set it on the kitchen counter. An overwhelming urge came over Janie to investigate what had his attention so gripped. She knew his PIN, but she had never felt compelled to use it, until that moment. She waited until he was situated under his truck, and when she saw the coast was clear, she went over to his phone. With trepidation, she entered the four numbers, gaining access to his virtual world. She quickly skimmed through his phone–her heart pounded rapidly in her chest. No dating or hook-up apps–*whew,* she sighed a breath of relief. Next, she scrolled through his texts–no names she didn't recognize. Okay...so far, so good. She then went to his search history, and there it was. Instantly, she saw what had her husband captivated.

Search after search result revealed Eddy's overenthusiasm for porn. Curiosity took over, and she opened a couple tabs. Wait...*what?* Live webcam girls? Janie felt like her heart was going to pound out of her chest. This wasn't a genre of videos they ever watched together–these weren't even recorded. Did this even classify as porn anymore? These were live shows of women masturbating in real-time. This entertainment platform was equivalent to Broadway adaptations of cinematic films. Janie was blown away.

She sat down. Her stomach clenched in knots as she watched the comments fly back and forth between the entertainer and her riveted audience. While she stared in disbelief at Eddy's phone trying to process what she was witnessing, something else caught her eye... now what was *this?* Private shows for pay? The thought of Eddy watching porn by himself was devastating enough, but this was a whole different animal! Was he paying for private masturbation shows? If he was interacting with these women, was that considered cheating? She wasn't sure, but it certainly felt like a high level of betrayal to her. It took every ounce of self-control not to confront Eddy at that moment because she knew if she did, she would lose her shit, bigtime. She needed some time to figure out how she was going to handle this in a more diplomatic way than ripping off his balls.

Janie set Eddy's phone back on the counter and walked zombie-like to the bedroom, overcome by a flood of painful emotions. She felt deeply hurt and offended, she felt jealous and insecure, she felt inadequate and betrayed, and she felt sadness mixed with anger that Eddy would occupy himself with this type of entertainment. He was such a great guy...she never dreamed he would be involved in such questionable activity.

Janie wanted to be calm and collected when she confronted Eddy about her discovery, so she let several days pass before she approached him. Rehearsing the scene in her head, she was certain he could not possibly justify or defend his actions, and that it would be a one-sided confrontation, *er*...conversation. From her perspective, he was caught with his pants down and had some serious explaining to do. But when she sat him down, the *two-sided* conversation didn't pan-out exactly the way she expected.

Though she tried to remain composed, an accusatory and condescending tone dominated her voice as she expressed the deep betrayal she felt about him watching porn–specifically, live webcam shows. She demanded an explanation, and it better be good. She asked him, "How could you go behind my back and satisfy yourself to other women? Why would you even seek that kind of entertainment? Are you paying for private masturbation shows?" She thought Eddy would sit in silence and take the verbal lashing he deserved, but when she gave him the window of opportunity to *dare* defend himself, his reply was not an easy pill for Janie to swallow.

Years of pent-up frustration and unexpressed emotions about their virtually non-existent sex life were now front and center, and Eddy could no longer avoid the subject. He began with what he considered the secondary issue. He explained to Janie that live webcam shows were no different than regular porn because he didn't pay for private shows–he was just a sideline observer. He showed Janie his credit card statements to prove he wasn't paying for personal entertainment. Although she was relieved he wasn't engaging in one-on-one interactions, she made it clear she didn't appreciate him pleasuring himself to ANY type of porn–live *or* recorded.

Now to address the primary issue Eddy quietly struggled with for the past few years. This was tough because he wasn't a confrontational guy, and he didn't know how explain his dissatisfaction without sounding selfish or accusatory. He mustered enough courage to utter the words, "Having sex only twice a month isn't enough for me." He continued, "Since you went through menopause, I've been sexually unsatisfied, and that's why I started watching porn. I have physical needs that aren't being met, and because I would never cheat on you, satisfying myself to porn seemed like a reasonable option." He went on to explain that he never wanted to say anything about their sex life because he understood she didn't have control over her body's changes. He expressed his deep regret that his lack of communication created this whole other issue and was sincerely apologetic for causing her so much pain.

Janie wished Eddy would have communicated his discontent with their sex life. If he had, perhaps they wouldn't be sitting there hashing-out this issue. As she listened to Eddy, she realized it never dawned on her that her declined sex drive didn't automatically convert to a declined sex drive for him. She assumed he was okay with the downward shift in sexual activity because he never said anything. But that was an incorrect assumption because thinking about it now, Eddy always had a high sex drive. It just never crossed her mind that her diminished interest had affected him so greatly. Janie apologized for her assumption, and they both agreed this was a topic they should have openly communicated about long ago.

Although Janie opposed Eddy's use of porn to fill their intimacy gap, she was wise enough to understand how he could convince himself it was an acceptable alternative to satisfy his physical needs, in the absence of an active sex life.

* * *

Now comes the question that begs to be answered...has pornography appeared in your life as a welcome guest or an unwelcome intruder? Based on the percentage of men who watch adult videos, there's a strong chance it plays some type of role in your relationship. For some couples, it works wonders to spice up their sex lives. For others, it doesn't, because one partner is against it, as you just read in the story above.

If you *are* open to watching adult videos as a prelude to sex, but haven't discussed the topic, open the conversation. If he's receptive, suggest that you'd like to watch videos as part of foreplay the next time you get together. I don't know your man, but if he's a proponent, there's a good chance he'll be excited about the idea. Couples should be open about this topic because if he's sneaky and watches them behind your back (or even blatantly in front of your face), it can create some big issues.

I believe men who rely on porn to fill the intimacy gap would reduce the amount of this solo activity if there was an increase in sexual activity, or if they knew their partner was open to watching videos to become sexually aroused together.

Honest Assessment

1. Have you ever enjoyed roleplay with your partner? If so, what scenarios?

YES / NO

2. Have you ever shared a fantasy with him, verbally or physically? If so, what was his reaction?

YES / NO

3. Do you own any sex toys?

YES / NO

4. If you answered no to any of the questions above, have you at least been curious?

____

____

____

5. Have you ever read erotica? If so, did it arouse you?

YES / NO

6. Have you ever lived out a fantasy? If so, was it amazing or underwhelming?

YES / NO

7. Do you ever incorporate any of the above ideas to sprinkle a little spice into your sex life?

YES / SOMETIMES / NO

8. Is your partner open or closed-minded? How about you?

____

____

____

9. Are you willing to step outside your comfort zone and explore any of the ideas in this chapter?

YES / MAYBE / NO

(If you oppose adult entertainment, skip questions 10-13)

10. Have you ever watched adult videos with or without your partner?

YES / NO

11. Do you know if he watches them without you?

HE DOES / HE DOESN'T / I DON'T KNOW

12. What are your general thoughts and opinions about watching adult videos? Do they offend or excite you?

____

____

____

13. If you never have, would you consider watching videos with your partner?

YES / MAYBE / NO

* * *

You've got your work cut out for you in this chapter. You have not one, not two, but up to **FIVE** Sexercises to complete!

Five? I know, I'm getting more demanding as we near the end of this guide. But I think you should expand your mind and try new things, especially if you haven't yet or you haven't done anything out of the ordinary in a long time. Try to complete these five Sexercises over the next several weeks to break things up and to avoid giving your partner a heart attack.

Sexercise One: Create A Roleplay Scenario

Think of a roleplay scenario you and your partner would enjoy. I'm sure he's made an innuendo at some point about seeing you dressed up as a fantasy character. But if not, choose something you think he'd like or you'd be able to play off well. The **Sexual Intimacy Ideas** in the back of the guide has lots of roleplay suggestions. And remember, own your character, be confident and bold, and be someone completely different from your personality. Refer to the **Roleplay Tips** at the beginning of the chapter, and most of all, enjoy the experience!

Sexercise Two: Tell A Bedtime Story

Here we go! This is the Sexercise I mentioned in the *Fantasies* section of this chapter. Choose one of your fantasies to create an erotica story to tell your partner. If you feel reluctant to share one of yours, ask him to share one of his during a post-sex talk. Believe me, he'll tell you! He may not be very descriptive but that's okay, you'll just have to build a story around the information he offers. If you say, "Honey, tell me one of your fantasies," he'll probably bullet point and say, "Redhead, blond, and me in a hot tub." Just take the information he gives and create the storyline yourself. You can also use content from other erotica stories for ideas. Run through the storyline in your head, visualize the scenario, and speak what you envision.

When you're ready to execute this Sexercise, set the mood with dim lighting, use a soft tone when you speak, and wear something seductive or nothing at all (except maybe his favorite perfume). Tell him to close his eyes or use an eye mask so his other senses become more heightened. Look over at him in five minutes or less and you'll see something standing at attention... guaranteed! Caress his body and stroke him while you're reading or telling your story. Be prepared for an awesome sex session after you've finished your tall tale.

Here's an example of how this Sexercise should play out. **WARNING! I am sharing with you an erotica story I've shared with my husband for our own fantasy experience. It contains graphic details and language, as only steamy erotica should. I'm just giving you the option to skip if sexually explicit details and language isn't your cup of tea.**

Otherwise...please read and enjoy my bedtime story!

The Bank

It was nighttime, and the kids were tucked away in their beds upstairs...far, far away from our *Fantasy Land.* My husband and I lay in bed, freshly showered and naked.

The room was lit with the soft glow of a single candle on my nightstand. He moved closer to me, his body now touching mine. He began tracing his fingers around my nipples. I lay still with my eyes closed, soaking in the sensation of his soft and smooth fingers. I opened my eyes and looked up at him, smirked, and looked away with a small smile on my lips.

"What are you smiling about?" he said.

"Do you want to hear a fantasy I experienced a long time ago?" I replied in a soft voice.

"Yes, tell me...I want to hear it," he whispered back.

And so, I began. I kept my voice soft and seductive while I told my tale...

When I was around 25, my girlfriend Zoe and I went to this awesome nightclub in Philadelphia called The Bank. The building was an old bank built in the late 1800s. But after the bank closed, it was converted into a nightclub. It had four levels with different style clubs on each floor. We eventually made our way down to the lowest level, the basement. It had a dungeon-like atmosphere. The old stone and mortared walls were dimly lit by fire torches, and red light cast down onto the concrete floor hidden from somewhere up in the ceiling. There were oversized, velvet lounges scattered throughout the maze of different rooms that beckoned you to sit down and get ultra-relaxed.

We wandered around, drinks in hand, with no particular destination. We were exploring the different rooms on our journey to nowhere. At the end of one hall were these huge, metal, cathedral-style doors. A sign above the doorway read "The Vault." There were several pieces of the same lounge furniture in that room as well. In a corner, on a big red chaise lounge, was a couple making out intensely. They were in their own world and didn't notice us standing in the doorway watching them. Zoe nudged me and said, "Damn, that's so hot, isn't it? They must not care if they're being watched. Maybe they like that...maybe they're exhibitionists!" I agreed. Maybe they were exhibitionists, or maybe they were just too wasted to care if they had an audience. I also agreed how hot it was watching this couple devour each other with such passion, alcohol-induced or not.

Over the loud techno music blasting from who-knows-where, Zoe told me she would get us a couple more drinks. I was already feeling the effects of the alcohol, but I was having such a good time and feeling pretty loose, so I said okay to one more drink. She made her way back down the hall to the bar as I stood there, leaning my shoulder against the doorway.

I was flat out staring at these two lovers in the corner. The girl was straddling the guy and facing in my direction, so his back was towards me. He had his shirt off and her shirt was pulled above her lacy black bra. I must have caught her eye while I was standing there because she glanced in my direction a couple of times while she was kissing his neck. She gave me a suggestive little half-smile, grabbing the side of her lower lip with her teeth and that tell-tale look in her eyes. I didn't walk away. I couldn't even look away. The sexy scene mesmerized me. I smiled back and kind of raised my eyebrows up as if to say, "I'd love to join your little party in the corner."

She whispered in the guy's ear, and he turned his head around towards me for just a second and then turned back towards her and nodded his head. She looked at me again, and with one finger, she gave me the "come here" signal. With curiosity, combined with my slightly impaired judgment from the alcohol, I began walking over to them. It was as if I were in a trance–I couldn't stop myself. She reached her hand out and grabbed mine to pull me towards them. The guy moved back to make room for me to sit right in front of him.

I faced her with my back against the guy's muscular chest. She and I began to kiss, our tongues softly exploring each other's wet mouths and juicy lips. The guy reached around, pulled down my low-cut top, and started squeezing my nipples and cupping my tits. The girl bent down and started to lick and suck one nipple while the guy still had my other nipple between his fingers, squeezing it hard. I let out a small whimper of pain, but he didn't stop. I didn't want him to because a tingling sensation of pleasure-pain shot straight down to my pussy.

The girl told the guy to move back farther, so he was sitting against the back of the lounge chair. She told me to lie down and put my head in his lap. I complied. I didn't have any underwear on, so when she pushed my miniskirt up to my hips, she had open access to my wet pussy. She started slowly licking and sucking around my clit. She gently spread my pussy lips apart with two fingers, then plunged her tongue deep inside of me. I could feel her tongue twirling around the outside and then she would suck on my whole pussy. I was dying. I never experienced a woman touching me before, say nothing about licking my pussy, but it felt incredible. Her tongue moved back up, dancing lightly around my clit in circles and then sucking on it, causing my whole body to spasm in deep pleasure.

Meanwhile, the guy still played with my nipples, but several times his arm reached over the top of my body to stick his fingers deep into my pussy. The girl got up from between my legs and leaned forward to give me a long and deep kiss. I could taste my sweet pussy juice from her mouth. It was so hot. She whispered in my ear, "Get doggy."

I did as I was told. She got next to me in the same position and pulled her skirt up around her hips like mine. The guy stood up behind the two of us as she and I began making out again. Our tongues went wild with desire. I felt him place his hands on my ass cheeks and before I knew it, I felt him drive his cock deep inside of me. I let out a loud moan, but I didn't care. It felt so good. He fucked me for a minute or two, then he pulled out and fucked her, taking turns, enjoying both of our hot pussies. While he was fucking her, he was feverishly rubbing my clit. She and I never stopped kissing the whole time he was taking turns fucking us. He finally came inside of her and after he did, he flopped down on a chair close to the chaise lounge we used as our makeshift bed.

She told me to lie down on the lounge and spread my legs. She got on top of me and straddled me so that her pussy was directly on top of mine. We started grinding our pussies together in a sensual frenzy. I had my hands on her hips, and she was kind of sitting up leaning forward, grabbing my tits. I could feel my clit rubbing directly on hers as we got into a rhythm. Our bodies moved amazingly in sync. I couldn't take it anymore...I could feel my orgasm building. My body was in such a state of ecstasy when I started, I heard myself crying out, "I'm gonna come, I'm gonna come!" She too started to breathe heavier at the same time saying, "I'm coming too...fuck! I'm coming too!"

I couldn't believe I actually had that experience. It felt so surreal. After we recovered from our exhaustion, I stood up and readjusted my skirt and top back to where they belonged. I looked over at the doorway where Zoe was standing with a drink in each hand, looking stunned and staring at me in complete disbelief. I turned around and with a shy closed-lipped smile, tilted my head in a nod of thanks to the girl and the guy. I turned back and walked over to my dumbfounded friend and grabbed my drink from her hand. As we walked back down the hall towards the main club upstairs, all she kept muttering was, "Oh my god, Em... oh my...what the...what the hell just happened?"

* * *

The only real part of my erotica was the atmosphere of a club I went to forever ago. The rest was just made up from a fantasy. Immediately after I was done telling my story, we had crazy, passionate sex because the juicy details and excitement had gotten us both so worked up.

Now it's your turn! Use your I-M-A-G-I-N-A-T-I-O-N to tell your man a hot and steamy story. If you feel it might be a stretch to create a story from a fantasy, you can share with him the erotica you wrote back in Key Eight: Power of the Mind...Magic of the Moment. Alternatively, if you feel just too out of your water with this Sexercise, drop it back a notch by reading other people's erotica stories you find online. You don't even have to read aloud if that doesn't feel comfortable. You can still be next to each other and choose erotica genres you individually find exciting to read to yourselves.

There are several variations to choose from depending on your comfort level. However, if you still feel hesitant to execute any variant of this Sexercise, tuck it away for a future idea as you become more sexually adventurous.

Sexercise Three: Buy A Sex Toy

If you're bold (and I believe you are, or you're at least well on your way), take a ride to your local adult toy shop (there's a good chance there's one in your town or in a town close by) and shop around for a sex toy and sexy wear.

If you're too shy or prefer to shop online, then visit my store **www.simtoyshop.com.** If you make a purchase, please know the packaging is completely discreet. No one will ever know you ordered a 10-inch purple vibrating double-dong dildo unless someone opens the package without your permission. In that case, you'll have some explaining to do, so you better be a good storyteller!

Online shopping for this type of purchase is great because it offers complete discretion. Having said that, I'd like to encourage you to go to an adult toy store at least once. Why? Well, because there's nothing to feel ashamed or embarrassed about! There's absolutely nothing wrong with buying a sex toy. Set your hesitation aside and feel confident and bold when you walk into that toy store. Believe me, the clerk will not judge you, nor will other like-minded people who are there to buy the same type of products. If you're unsure what to look for, start out in sexy wear and then make your way over to the vibrator section. There's a wide array of vibrators to choose from so buy something different from what you already own. If this is your first sex toy, buy yourself either a rabbit or clitoral vibrator with varying speeds. To be honest, you really can't go wrong with any type of vibrator!

It's fun and liberating to feel uninhibited about sexual exploration, even if you don't wind up buying anything. You can do this Sexercise together with your partner if you think he'd enjoy the shopping trip, or go alone to surprise him, or go with a girlfriend. You ladies will have a blast! It's your call.

(If you oppose adult entertainment, skip Sexercise Four)

Sexercise Four: Watch Adult Videos Together

Since I created this guide to help expand your sexual horizons, then why not do just that? Jump in the deep end! Watch some adult videos together with your partner. Visit an adult website and explore genres you think you'd enjoy watching together. Because the world of adult videos is virtually limitless, there are many categories, including female-friendly, where the videos are softer and more romantic in nature. If you find it challenging to choose a specific genre you both would enjoy, you don't have to watch the same videos. You can still be next to each other but on your own devices. Peruse through the categories and choose your personal preferences.

Whether you watch the same videos together or watch your own videos next to each other, he'll be so excited he won't know what to do with himself. You should be close enough so you can play with each other while watching videos. This Sexercise can and should lead to some super-hot and exciting sex. If you've never done this, you'll immediately see what I'm talking about!

Sexercise Five: Make Your Own Adult Video

If you're not comfortable or fully convinced watching other people having sex is your thing, that's okay! You can still enjoy the concept without watching other people *per se.* Why not create your own video? That's right! Here are a few different ways to be the star of your own movie.

Use your camera recorder on your cell phone. It's easy to hold and move around, and you can get some awesome close-up angles. You can also use a Go-Pro with a short handle so you can get a little further away from the action. Another idea is setting up a video recorder on a tripod. If you have a photo light, the bright light helps create a quality show. If you don't want to record your steamy flick, your last option would be to set a full-length mirror close to the bed or position yourself in front of it and watch. That's a lot of fun too!

The alternative options in this Sexercise shows you don't have to compromise any of your personal values if you feel conflicted about watching adult videos. As you can see, there are many other ways to enjoy the concept without watching other people. I feel certain your man will thoroughly enjoy any of the above listed ways you try.

If you've never explored any of these types of sexual adventures, now is a great time to expand your horizons and open yourself up to different ways that will unquestionably improve your sex life with your partner. Remove mental blocks or reservations you may have and at least *try* some suggestions in this chapter. I think you'll be pleasantly surprised to learn how these pleasurable and exciting experiences can bring a huge burst of sexual energy into your relationship.

My SIM Journal

After you've completed all your Sexercises, write about each experience. First, reflect on what you felt during the preparation for each Sexercise. Did you feel nervous or excited? Were you filled with sexual anticipation?

Now write a summary about all these experiences. How did this type of sexual exploration feel? Were you fully engaged in your character/story/toy/video? Did you feel awkward or like a sex vixen? How did your partner respond to these Sexercises? Was he onboard or did he seem uninterested? At the beginning of this guide, we discussed unspoken communication. What was his body language telling you during these Sexercises?

The Key to Fantasy Land

Open willingness to explore sexual adventures outside your normal routine is the key to Fantasy Land. Remember, anything you introduce that you have a true desire to explore will naturally create arousal and anticipation.

KEY TEN
Don't Just Appease ... *Please!*

It's Saturday afternoon. You're lounging around the house because it's cold and rainy outside. Laying low is normal on a day like this...it's a free pass to chill. Your sister picked up your kids to play with their cousins, so you and your man have a few unexpected hours alone. You're contemplating the best way to take advantage of this precious time without the kids because it's such a rare event.

What are YOUR thoughts?

A. Oh boy, maybe I'll take a two-hour uninterrupted nap. Yay!

B. This house is such a mess...I should clean this afternoon since the kids aren't here. I can get a lot accomplished.

C. I have that damn work project and my deadline's just about here...I should probably work on it today since I have the time.

D. Maybe I'll take this opportunity to go shopping. I need to get some groceries and there's a great shoe sale at Macy's I'd hate to miss.

What are HIS thoughts?

A. I know she'll probably take a nap because the kids aren't here, but I want to lie in bed, have sex, and enjoy each other.

B. She'll probably want to clean the house, but I want to lie in bed, have sex, and enjoy each other.

C. I bet she'll get into her work project because her deadline is close, but I want to lie in bed, have sex, and enjoy each other.

D. She might want to go out shopping, but I want to lie in bed, have sex, and enjoy each other.

I bet I'm not far off the mark in this scenario of how women and men think so differently. If you *were* so lucky to have a day as described, would the idea of lying in bed, having sex, and enjoying each other even cross your mind?

- ☐ Definitely
- ☐ Maybe
- ☐ Not a chance

Passive or Aggressive?

Do you ever initiate sex, or is it always him? If he's the one always in hot pursuit, you must make a change, my friend. I've only learned the importance of this key ingredient to a healthy and balanced sex life in my current marriage. I can't believe I didn't figure this out much earlier. Like myself, I believe many women unintentionally overlook the importance of initiating sex. However, you must understand how essential this gesture is to your partner.

The act of initiating intimacy is something most women don't even pay attention to and yet, it's one of the most important and vital elements a man desires from his woman.

My husband is a very sexual man and would happily have sex every day if left entirely up to him. Although I'm always available to meet his sexual needs, as in, I never reject him unless I have a *legitimate* headache, that level of availability and willingness only counts to a point. You may think, *If you never reject him then clearly, you're always meeting his needs. How could that not be satisfactory? What more could he possibly want?*

I asked myself the same questions, believe me. I'm pretty sure there aren't too many men in long-term relationships who can say they still have sex multiple times a week after so many years together. I was baffled by his dissatisfaction with our active sex life, so we talked. Come to find out, being available to fulfill his sexual needs whenever he wanted wasn't the ticket. I was floored. *How could this be?* Well, because *he* always had to pursue *me* for sex.

Wait, wait, wait a minute here. Not only did he want to have sex every day, but he also wanted *me* to pursue *him?* Was he crazy? Surely, he'd lost his mind. I mean, was he serious? Yes, he was. After some in-depth conversations, I now understand that when I pursue him, it deeply satisfies his need to feel what all men long to feel: desired.

It was a hard realization that being available to have sex any time he wanted wasn't the point. I won't lie, I felt a tremendous letdown. I thought I was knocking it out of the park, and in a way I was, but not completely. Instead of becoming defensive and dismissive, I set my ego aside and tried to gain a better understanding of his perspective. If he truly longs to feel desired by me, then of course he would feel more satisfied when I initiated sex.

Thankfully, we have excellent open communication, so he could articulate the importance of this issue. I could then work to improve this part of our sexual intimacy. This is a perfect example of why open communication is so crucial. If he didn't explain this feeling of lack, I would have mistakenly continued to believe I was fully satisfying his needs, when I actually wasn't. I would've never known, and I wouldn't have been able to do anything to improve the situation. Because he took the time and effort to express his needs, I can now say that I completely understand the importance of initiating sex. To be honest, I'd rather have the opportunity to step-up or change my game than have him ultimately decide to seek someone else to fill that void and make him feel desired, as many men do.

Having said all that, I have to level with you. Even though I fully understand my husband's desire for me to pursue him, to this day, it's still a push to stay mindful of this need. I've gotten better, but there's still room for improvement. I was so accustomed to him being the one pursuing me for so many years. If I don't set my intention to pursue him for sex, it won't happen.

At the beginning of our relationship, there was no need to think about this issue; in fact, it was a complete non-issue. I was a prowling tigress, *always* pursuing him. He couldn't keep me off him, literally. I was a wild woman who sought to have sex multiple times a day. There's no doubt in my mind I put his abilities to the test. This was during the Bliss Zone everyone experiences when they're with a new person. But as the years roll on, and overwhelming, ravenous desire for sex simmers down during the Comfort Zone, being the pursuer can easily fall to the wayside, as it did for me.

In the infancy of a relationship, it's effortless for the woman to initiate sex, often. We're beyond capable of being insatiable creatures. I think we even surprise ourselves sometimes how much sexual energy and vigor we can have with a new partner. Although I'm still incredibly attracted to my husband and thoroughly enjoy our bond of sexual intimacy, maintaining this one aspect of our sexual relationship hasn't come easy for me. I no longer have the help of raging hormones and chemicals rushing through my body or the excitement of being with someone new creating the desire to hunt him down for a sexual encounter.

If you're in a similar situation, it probably hasn't come easy for you either. It's a difficult pattern to change because it's breaking a habit, so to speak. However, it's necessary to change this pattern so you can improve this area of sexual intimacy. Unfortunately, I don't believe my husband is the only man who struggles with this issue. Many men feel a void in this area of their relationship because they too have a strong need to feel desired and pursued by their women, but often their needs are unintentionally (or intentionally) overlooked or ignored. To make matters worse, men can have a harder time expressing their feelings and communicating issues with their partner.

Why not exercise your empathy muscle for a moment? Imagine you were the one in your relationship with a high or even average sex drive, but he always ignored your need for sexual intimacy. If you always had to be the initiator of sex because he didn't seem interested either way, how would that make you feel? Wouldn't you long for him to pursue you once in a while to satisfy your need to feel desired, without it resembling a cat-and-mouse chase? Or feeling like you have to beg or bargain to have sex? You would yearn for your man to pursue you for a sexual encounter, at least occasionally.

Since men are typically the initiators of sex, most women never experience this issue because their needs of feeling desired are being met. Therefore, many women can't relate to the feelings of neglect, rejection, and dissatisfaction men experience by not being pursued, simply because they don't have the opportunity to experience these feelings themselves.

If you're in a routine where your man is the one always looking for you, be mindful of his need to feel desired, and work towards *occasionally* seeking him. I'm not suggesting you chase him down for sex every day like at the beginning of your relationship. That's far from realistic. But increase your effort from wherever it is now. So, if it's never, make it once a month. If it's once a month, make it twice a month, and so on. Now you know beyond the shadow of a doubt what your man needs from you. Do your part and give him what he wants, which is feeling desired by you. Even if he hasn't brought this to your attention, trust me, it's something he would love to see happen.

When you make the move to pursue your man, your excitement and desire must feel authentic. If it's not, he'll sense you're only going through the motions and that won't make him feel desirable at all, will it? You must actively seek ways to excite yourself because sexual energy is something you cannot fake–either you feel it, or you don't. Look through the list of ideas below to help build sexual arousal prior to your pursuit:

- Read erotica, naked.
- Watch your favorite categories of adult videos, but don't play with yourself.
- Engage in sexting with your man all afternoon.
- Masturbate with or without sex toys, but not to climax.
- Wear a bra and panty set that makes you feel super sexy.

- Take a relaxing bubble bath or shower, shave your legs and your pubic area. When you're done, lather your whole body with a silky soft after-shower lotion or powder.
- Walk around the house naked or wear a short, sexy robe or lingerie.
- Wear a pair of vibrating or crotchless panties while you read erotica/watch videos, or even when you're going about your day.
- Take the time to make yourself look beautiful and desirable–hair, nails, makeup, etc.
- Wear clothing that makes you feel incredibly sexy. Look in the mirror and admire your reflection.
- Visualize how you want your pursuit to play out while pleasuring yourself.
- Prepare your bedroom with whatever elements you will use later (i.e., candles, aromatherapy, sex toys, massage oil, etc.).

Think Sexy to Feel Sexy

The trick to experience genuine excitement to pursue your partner is this: you must *think* sexy to feel sexy. When you feel sexy, your desire for intimacy should naturally increase. For example, if you put on a sexy panty and bra set, don't go about your business and forget what you're wearing under your clothes. **Think** about how sexy you look in your panties, how good the material feels on your vagina, and how awesome the style compliments your booty. **Think** about how enticing your cleavage looks in your bra and imagine your man's excitement when he sees you wearing your sexy undergarments.

Or when you've finished reading a steamy erotica, turn your physical stimulation into **thoughts** about your upcoming sexual pursuit. **Think** about what sexy attire you're going to wear that makes your body look smoking hot. When you take a shower, feel your silky-smooth shaved legs and pubic area, and imagine your man enjoying the smoothness of your skin. Also, **think** about details of the erotica you read. Which parts made you feel exceptionally horny? Replay those scenes in your mind to keep your arousal level elevated for your sexual encounter.

What differentiates a going-through-the-motions sexual experience from a fully engaged and passionate sexual experience is your thought process. In addition to sexy and sensual thoughts, women in long-term relationships should utilize sexual aides like sexy wear, sex toys, erotica, etc., to get excited about having sex. ***THERE IS UNEQUIVOCALLY NO SHAME IN USING ANY MEANS NECESSARY TO HELP YOURSELF BECOME***

AROUSED! (That was me shouting into my bullhorn from the rooftop.) As long as your buildup of excitement converts into pursuing your partner and having a great time, there's nothing wrong with using sexual aides to help in the process–that's exactly their purpose! When I combine one of the above ideas with sexy wear that makes me feel hot and sensual, it's a surefire way to get me going...every time.

Don't Miss the Mark!

After my husband initially brought this whole pursuit issue to my attention, the first time I tried to initiate sex after being out of practice for so long, I misunderstood "I want you to pursue me" and thought he wanted me to act like an aggressive, take-charge dominatrix, which are the farthest characteristics from my personality. My attempt felt so contrived and phony and so not me. Strong parts of my personality include shyness and being laid back, so I felt beyond awkward trying to act like a hardcore seductress when clearly, I was not.

Well, I missed the mark again. Approaching him with a different personality wasn't what he wanted. While pretending to be someone different works great for roleplay, this wasn't a roleplay situation. My approach should have been more organic. For my personality, the scenario would have resembled something more like this: look at him shyly, flirt with my eyes and my lips, and sit on his lap for a meaningful hug. Then softly kiss his lips and neck, stand up, take his hand, and lead him to the bedroom. Not only did I feel totally awkward when I tried to approach him like a boss, but he could also sense how uncomfortable I felt. When you approach your man, choose a method that comes naturally. If you're a wild tigress, be a wild tigress. But if you're more like a docile kitty cat, then come to him like the docile kitty cat you are.

The Right Time

When you plan your pursuit, aim for morning time, the kids' nap time, or right after they go to sleep, rather than your bedtime. If you're anything like me, the only thing you want to pursue at the end of a long day is your favorite sleeping position. Do you often reject your man because you don't want to do ANYTHING when you crawl into bed, except close your eyes? It can cause inner conflict if you want to satisfy him but feel so overwhelmingly tired that your brain can't register anything else at that point but the need to sleep. You'll feel very accomplished when you get into bed knowing you've already pursued and pleased your man.

On the other hand, if you're one of the few women who has energy reserves when you get into bed at night, this advice doesn't apply to you. But to the 99.9 percent of other women who just have nothing left to give by the end of a long day...do not put unnecessary pressure on yourself.

Let me throw this in while we're hashing out the most opportune time for your pursuit. During a post-sex conversation, discuss the frequency of sex you agree is a reasonable amount during the week/month that works for *both of you.* This way, you can avoid feelings of guilt because you're not being put in the position to deny him, and he doesn't have to feel rejected or neglected by you, because you've already set the expectation. Compromise and reach a mutual agreement on what will work best and be sure to initiate sex at least once a month.

The woman being the pursuer is a monumentally huge deal and incredibly important to most men out there, probably including yours. Mark my words, this effort on your part will go a long way.

Please Him

The goal in this chapter is not only to make you aware of the importance of pursuing your man, but also how to ***please*** him. Think about it for a moment...what makes your man tick? What makes him excited? Are you unconsciously denying him certain pleasures? Is there a chance some sexual and non-sexual treats he once enjoyed are no longer on the menu? If so, consider offering these long-forgotten treats to him again. Or if you want to explore new ways to show your love, look through the **Sexual Intimacy Ideas** in the back of the guide so you don't have to wrack your brain.

Would you agree the gesture of pleasing another person is a selfless act? It means we sometimes do things we don't necessarily *want* to do, but we do them anyway because the ultimate goal is to make the other person happy. If he enjoys when you wear something sexy to bed, wear something sexy. If he expresses the desire to spend more quality time you, find the time to make it happen. If cooking a big Sunday breakfast makes him feel happy, then whip up those eggs with love on Sunday mornings. If you're not really sure...then *ask* him! He will highly appreciate your efforts, and your willingness to please him will make him feel very special.

Here's a short story of an extremely grateful and excited reaction I received for a teeny-tiny act of thoughtfulness. A few weeks ago, Angel was getting ready to go running at the park. I asked him if he wanted anything to eat for dinner when he got home. He said not to worry about cooking and that he would just grab some fruit. Yay for me! I didn't have to cook! But then I thought about how easy-going he always is when it comes to mealtime. So, I decided to be nice and prepare the fruit for him (even though I hate cutting up fruit). I didn't just cut up the fruit and throw it all together in a bowl. Oh no...I went a step further and made a layered, decorative fruit display. I even impressed myself with how pretty it looked. When he got home and opened the fridge door and saw the lovely fruit plate, well, I'm telling you, you would've thought I surprised him with a Rolex watch or a winning lottery ticket. He was over-the-top thrilled and so appreciative. He went on and on about the beautiful fruit plate, what an amazing and thoughtful wife I am, how special that made him feel, what a lucky man his is, and how it was one of the nicest things anyone has ever done for him. Wow! His huge, gratitude-filled response was all for less than 15 minutes of my time and effort. Based on my experience with this scenario and other small efforts I've made to show my husband I love him, it seems like it's the little gestures that can make a man feel the most special and loved.

When you take time to please your partner, whether it's on or off the bed, it lets him know you care about his happiness. When he sees you're attempting to satisfy his wants and needs, you also send him the unspoken message that you still truly love him. It's our human nature to want to feel special, desired, and loved, isn't it? If you work hard to show your partner ways to make him feel that, I believe he will reciprocate the same gestures back to you—it's contagious.

I established at the beginning, and have repeated throughout this guide, that my mission is to help *you* actively reestablish the bond of sexual intimacy with your partner. In order to reestablish this bond, you must think from the perspective of "What can *I* do to improve our sex life and overall relationship? What can *I* do to strengthen and renew our connection?" You want him to feel like his woman has come back to life, filled with passion and excitement. If you put forth the effort to please him the way you did in the Bliss Zone, he will undoubtedly be a very willing participant in the rebirth of your bond of sexual intimacy.

You have the choice to create any cycle you want in your relationship, good *or* bad. If you give me what I need, I'll give you what you need. *We'll be happy.* If you don't give me what I need, I won't give you what you need. *We'll be miserable.* You both must compromise and work together if you sincerely want to rebuild a strong and enjoyable relationship.

Honest Assessment

1. Do you ever pursue your man to be sexually intimate?

YES / SOMETIMES / NEVER

2. If so, when was the last time you were the pursuer? If not, what is/are the reason(s) you don't pursue him?

____

____

____

3. Did you pursue your man often at the beginning of your relationship? If so, would you say that's decreased over the years?

YES / SOMETIMES / NO

4. Has he ever expressed to you his need to feel pursued or desired by you?

YES / SOMETIMES / NO

If you answered yes, have you ignored his requests, or have you done anything to improve this aspect of your sexual relationship?

____

____

____

5. Do you have a scheduled routine for sex, or does it happen spontaneously?

____

____

____

6. When and what was the last nice gesture you made to please your man? Was it from the kindness of your heart? Guilt? Habit? Just because?

____

____

____

7. If it's been too long to remember the last nice gesture you showed your man, why do you suppose that is?

____

____

____

8. Does he still try to please you in any of the ways he did at the beginning of your relationship? If not, why do you think he stopped?

YES / SOMETIMES / NO

____

____

____

9. Has your desire to pursue or please your man after reading through most of this guide increased at all? Why or why not?

YES / SOMEWHAT / NOT REALLY

____

____

____

Sexercise One: Pursue Your Man!

Now you know beyond the shadow of a doubt the importance of pursuing your man, so it's time to execute a plan of action!

PLAN A

Pick a weekend night for your hot pursuit. He will believe you're being spontaneous, but in reality, you're not. Plan at least the highlights. *On Saturday night, I'll wear my new sexy nighty under my robe, and right after the kids go to bed, I'll sneak out to the car. I'll text him and tell him I need his help to get something out of the car. When he gets to the car, he'll see me sitting in the back seat with my new sexy nighty. I'll tell him to get in the car and* ________________. (Fill in the blank.)

PLAN B

The next time you see your partner in bed relaxing, go take a shower and when you're done, walk over to his side of the bed. Drop your towel, climb onto the bed, and situate yourself between his legs. Don't say a word. Pull down his pajama pants or underwear if he's wearing them and give him a *meaningful* BJ. When I say meaningful, I mean...be *juicy!* Get into the act! Prior to this nice little treat for your man, get yourself aroused, whatever that means for you personally.

Don't just go through the motions and act like you're doing him a solid. Take his penis in your mouth and enjoy it like you did in the Bliss Zone. Playfully dance your tongue around the tip, go down his shaft as far as you can, then come back up and suck on the tip this time. Spend a few minutes around his groin area kissing and licking around the base of his shaft. Lick his penis from the bottom to the top, then stroke it, varying your pressure with both hands. Show him you're completely into the act and thoroughly enjoying making him feel incredible. If you're fully immersed in the pleasure you're giving him, you will experience excitement within yourself, and before you know it, you'll be climbing aboard for a nice ride.

Pursuing him even once or twice a month will rekindle his excitement about this aspect of your relationship. You'll be adding such an important element back into the equation, which is making him feel special and desired by the woman he loves—you.

These are just a couple examples of being the pursuer. If these ideas don't float your boat, pull out some of your old tricks. I'm sure they'll work just as well. You can also research ideas online, look through **Sexual Intimacy Ideas** in the back of the guide, or get some ideas from one of your sassy girlfriends. We all have *at least* one great idea we're happy to share!

Sexercise Two: Please Your Man!

Think back to the beginning of your relationship. Do you remember all the sweet gestures you showed your man once upon a time? You were in *full impress mode* back then, so there's no doubt you will have some great ideas to pull from the archives. Start by choosing one or two gestures you know made him feel super special.

For example, the next time you're at the grocery store, pick up his favorite ice cream or snack food. Or as soon as he gets home and sits down from a long day, give him a nice shoulder massage. Or when you get into bed, give him a foot or full body massage. Or take a shower with him and lovingly wash his body, even his hair (if he still has any)! You know your man and what makes him feel happy and loved. Go ahead, show him gestures you know will make him feel just that...happy and loved. *And don't stop!* Get in the habit of pleasing him long after you complete this Sexercise. Think of a sweet or sexual gesture to make him feel special at least once a week. You will feel good by giving, and he will feel good from receiving.

I'm sure it feels like you're the one pulling all the weight and doing all the hard work through this journey, but remember, *you are the one* who has taken the initiative to hit the reset button in your relationship. To make a big change, it typically requires one person to acknowledge a change is needed, and that person takes the lead with the hope the other person will follow.

If you've made a genuine effort with your Sexercises, but he hasn't been fully receptive or responsive, step back and honestly assess the signals he's been sending regarding his feelings for you and your relationship. This is where you would mindfully observe his unspoken communication of body language and/or silence. But as long as he's still invested in your relationship, he will have happily taken part in these Sexercises meant to stimulate a rebirth of your relationship.

My SIM Journal

Write about the ways you pursued and pleased your partner at the beginning of your relationship. How do you believe these gestures made him feel? Write about how you think he may feel with the absence or serious reduction of these types of expressions of love. Be honest with yourself. Why do you think you no longer pursue him or show gestures to please him, if you don't? You have to understand the reasons and communicate them with him. Only then can you work on making changes to create more expressive and loving exchanges.

The Key to Don't Just Appease … *Please!*

When you step back and honestly assess your sexual interactions, what do you see? If he's the one always pursuing you, turn this around. Pursuing your man for sexual intimacy is the key to this chapter. Don't overlook this simple but highly effective way to make an immediate improvement in your relationship. While you're at it, don't forget to throw in those small but meaningful gestures to *please* your man to make him feel special again.

The Hard Truth

I'm going to level with you. Throughout writing this guide, I've gone back and forth with a real inner struggle of whether to include this chapter or not. I didn't want any content that might be perceived as negative or make anyone feel offended or conflicted. At the same time, one of the primary reasons I've worked tirelessly on creating this guide for women is actually *because* of the Hard Truth. Therefore, I cannot tiptoe around the topic. I would be withholding important information that belongs in this guide.

So fair warning...this chapter may touch you in ways that may not feel comfortable, and frankly, some information might make you feel like jumping out of your skin. But since my sincere intention is to be open and honest with you in a well-rounded manner, I must address this unfortunate place some long-term relationships land.

I hope you've learned enough about me through this journey to know my sole purpose and desire is to help you improve your relationship with your partner. I haven't written the content in this chapter to scare you, make you question your partner's integrity, or plant seeds of doubt in your mind. Nor have I written this chapter to make you feel ashamed or guilty if you've considered or have gone outside of your relationship to fill a void. My only intention is to make you aware of how a long-term relationship can easily wind up in the Danger Zone, which, as we know, is a breeding ground for some big, but avoidable problems.

The Initial Betrayal

Let's revisit the Bliss Zone in your relationship once again. Every action was effortless because you lived and breathed to satisfy, impress, and fill each other with happiness every moment of every day. Back then, whether you realized it, you both had certain **expectations** you believed would stay intact long after the ink dried on your marriage certificate, or from the time you began to live together. I'm sure you sincerely believed you could sustain a high level of interest and effort because you were so head-over-heels in love. It likely seemed impossible your interest in each other could ever wane.

I will ask you two questions now, and I want you to really think about your answers. Be honest with yourself. Do you feel *you've* lived up to his expectations of *you* in the relationship? And do you feel *he's* lived up to your expectations of *him*? My guess is there's a "no" or a "not quite" in there somewhere because you're reading this guide. There's some level of discontent or disconnect in the relationship on one or both sides.

Here's a couple examples of certain expectations I'm referring to. If you were insatiable at the beginning of your relationship and had sex every day of the week, but now 14 years later, you have sex only once a month, do you think he might feel betrayed or resentful because your sex life has declined so much? Is it fair to say his **expectation** was probably that he would have a fulfilling and active sex life based on your stamina and interest in sex at the beginning of your relationship?

What about his side? Did he shower you with affection, romance, and thoughtful gifts too often to keep track of when you first got together? Based on his attentiveness, you probably thought that special treatment could never end, but now even receiving a card on your birthday seems like a real effort on his behalf. The absence of affection and romantic gestures might make you feel you're no longer important to him or that he doesn't care about making you feel special anymore. If this is the case, how does that make you feel? Probably a bit discouraged and unsatisfied because he hasn't continued to fulfill your **expectations** of him.

Of course, it's unrealistic to maintain these relationship attributes as intensely as they were in the Bliss Zone, but there is a certain level of expectation that subconsciously remains long after that season in your relationship has passed. If one or both partners dramatically slacks or completely stops paying attention to these types of unspoken expectations, the red flag should fly up. As you've learned through this guide, the waning of focus on the relationship has a way of slowly breaking down communication and bonds between you. If you both lose focus and allow each other's expectations to become no longer important, you unintentionally open the door to many negative scenarios.

Unfortunately, men and women get discouraged because they've tried to communicate their dissatisfaction to their partner on several occasions, but to no avail. When people feel they've hit a communication wall, they sometimes believe that productive problem-solving and good communication occurs with someone outside their relationship, rather than with their partner.

This point is where the deception begins. Most of us have known at least one person who has cheated or is cheating but will never leave their partner because they know they're a good person. There's likely just a portion of the relationship that's missing. The dissatisfaction from that missing piece morphs into the justification to fulfill what's missing but with someone else.

There are countless statistics I could reference to show the prevalence of infidelity, but instead of delving into specific numbers and percentages, let's just look at an overview of what's available out there in our vast digital world. There are 2,500 dating sites alone in the U.S. and 8,000 worldwide, making the process to connect with other individuals *extremely* easy. These online platforms are not only useful for single people who are genuinely looking for love or even just a random hook-up, but also for committed people who want a quick and easy way to satisfy themselves with another person outside their relationship. As I'm sure you're aware, there are many cheating sites that offer like-minded people the platform to find others who want to go outside their relationship to enjoy a hook-up, fling, or affair.

How does this happen? How is it that when a person becomes *so frustrated* with their partner, they decide the remedy is to break the boundaries of their commitment? Well, I don't believe it's necessarily the intention or a calculated act, though there are circumstances where that's the case. But I believe when a person in a long-term relationship comes to their partner and puts their wants and needs on the table and they're ignored, this can be perceived as rejection or apathy.

For many people, it takes a lot of courage to go to their partner and articulate what's missing from the relationship, especially men. So, when a person comes to their partner and *wants* to do the right thing and their feelings are repeatedly disregarded, I think that's when a mental shift can occur. Maybe it feels like, "Hey, I've had many reasonable and heartfelt conversations with you to let you know what makes me feel unhappy in our relationship. If you ignore me and choose to not work on improving what is lacking, I will meet my needs with *or* without you." I know that seems cold, but the fact remains many people have sexual relations outside of their relationship, and not because they slipped and accidentally fell into someone else's bed.

I think for many men, the lack they feel in the relationship usually boils down to *not enough*. Not enough attention, not enough sex, or a combination of both. For women, I believe there's usually an emotional void that sends her off to seek another man willing to show her attention and make her feel special and adored.

In my quest to understand some of the real-deal reasons why both men *and* women cross their relationship boundaries, I performed my own informal polls. I asked a few male friends the top three reasons a man would ultimately go outside of his relationship. Here were the top three "justifiable" reasons (I said **top three**...there were more...*sigh*.):

1. Need to feel desired

Examples: Physical attention, a woman showing genuine interest in him and what he has to say, gives him compliments, makes him feel good about himself, and is excited to have sex with him.

2. No emotional baggage

Examples: No relationship history, no ongoing problems or issues, engaging in conversations about **non**-work/children/financial/relationship topics, and the thrill of something brand-new, fresh, and exciting.

3. Plain old narcissism

Men who need their egos stroked by anyone willing to stroke it. An insatiable need that cannot be quenched by one woman alone.

I conducted the same poll on some lady friends and coincidentally, most of the responses were strikingly similar.

1. Need to feel acknowledged

Examples: Engaging conversations, care/concern, receiving compliments, feeling valued and appreciated.

2. Need to feel desired

Examples: Compliments about appearance, affection, shows a genuine interest in her, makes her feel sexy, focuses on her pleasure, and makes her feel special.

3. Retribution

An eye for an eye...a tooth for a tooth. "Oh, so you want to cheat on me? Okay, well, two can play that game."

Here's a story of two couples whose relationships ended because of betrayal, a situation none of them ever believed could happen. These couples were suddenly faced with the fact that complacency had crept into their relationships, and ever so slowly, it had created a deep and widening wedge. Both couples were met with the huge realization their seemingly stable marriages had silently slipped into the Danger Zone, and their relationships were over long before they ended.

* * *

Alex and Laura fell in love and got married right after they graduated from college. The idea of having a big family excited them both, so within their first seven years of marriage, they had four children. Alex earned his degree in business administration, and over the years, he moved his way up to CFO of the company he worked for. Because Alex could financially provide for their family on his own, Laura stayed at home to raise their children.

They had a relatively normal life filled with soccer practices, dance lessons, school events, annual vacations to grandma's house and Disney World, and dinner every evening at 6 pm. Though their big family kept both Laura and Alex busy day and night, they tried to keep their relationship intact by staying sexually intimate once a week, celebrating their anniversary at their favorite restaurant every year, and always kissing goodbye before Alex went to work for the day.

As the years rolled on, their kids became tweens, teens, and finally flew from the nest. One by one, they went off to college. By the time their last child left home, Alex and Laura had spent 25 years together. Laura had built her identity around the role of a mother to her four children. But with them gone, she felt like she no longer had a purpose or an identity.

Their once lively home was now filled only with the sound of silence. No children to make breakfast for or drive to school, no sports games to cheer them on, and no more dirty laundry thrown on their bedroom floor to complain about for the eight-millionth time. Laura experienced the full blow of her empty nest and felt totally lost without her children to care for. In the silence of her long days alone, Laura began to realize her relationship with Alex had evolved basically into child-rearing partners over the years. They no longer had an emotional connection as a couple, and although they still had sex once a week after all their years together, she realized it was just part of the routine, a meaningless interaction.

Laura felt overwhelming unfulfillment and loneliness, and like the ocean, these feelings kept coming wave after wave. Because she placed all her focus and attention on her children, she inadvertently let important parts of their relationship slip away, and Alex, by default, followed her lead. They both unintentionally let the ship sink. Although she recognized there was nothing left to their relationship except an empty shell, she didn't feel any desire to make the necessary efforts it would take to restore their marriage.

Instead of dealing with this newly revealed issue she didn't feel compelled to tackle, she focused on herself and took part in activities she once enjoyed but had placed on the backburner. Pottery and private tennis lessons helped pass the time and kept her mind occupied. Her tennis instructor Dave was a friendly and handsome man in his early 50s with a great sense of humor. As the weeks went on, she noticed she felt especially excited about her lesson time with Dave and started spending extra time on her appearance before her lessons.

During her lesson time, their conversations went from polite and general to playful, serious, and even profound. As it turned out, Dave was a recent empty-nester too. Besides this relatable connection they shared, there was something about him that made her feel alive inside, something she hadn't felt in an awfully long time.

They enjoyed their conversations so much, they talked long after their lesson time was over and began to meet up for smoothies or coffee afterward so they could continue talking. The more they spoke, the more they learned about each other's personal lives, including their stagnated marriages. It became clear to Laura that Dave was in the same boat, an emotionally barren relationship that had stayed intact to raise their kids.

When Dave and Laura spent time together, they felt happy and fulfilled, and their feelings inevitably strengthened. As they shared more details about their mundane relationships, these discussions fueled their desire to be with someone who made them feel special and loved again.

These amazing feelings they experienced when they spent time together, intertwined with the unhappiness and dissatisfaction they both felt in their current relationships, became the green light for allowing their emotionally charged feelings for each other to take control. Having experienced these incredible feelings again after so many years in loveless relationships, it was easy for them to justify stepping outside the boundaries of their relationships. They assured each other and themselves that it was okay because there was no emotional connection left anyway, making it easier to play down the fact they were breaking their spousal commitments.

Dave and Laura decided they could not ignore the feelings they developed, and so they ended their relationships. The happiness, excitement, and love they were missing for so long made them feel it was the right choice to end their dead marriages. Even though this joint decision created an enormous upheaval in both their families, they felt it was ultimately the right decision to live the rest of their lives in happiness rather than in emptiness.

* * *

Can you see how easily complacency can infiltrate a relationship? Though not the only reason, this scenario is probably one of the most *common* reasons people in long-term relationships find themselves in this unintentional predicament. Most of the time couples are oblivious to the fact this slow and quiet decline is happening...until it's too late.

If both Dave and Laura had stayed mindfully aware of maintaining their important relationship bonds day after day and year after year with their respective partners, there's a strong possibility they wouldn't have experienced such a massive void in their relationships for someone else to come along and fill.

In other words, if they had kept their relationships solid by maintaining the Ten Keys necessary to sustain a healthy relationship, there's a good chance they wouldn't have reached the point of no return.

Honest Assessment

1. Do you think cheating is a forgivable or unforgivable act? Why or why not?

YES / UNDECIDED / NO WAY

2. Has betrayal happened in your current or a past relationship?

YES / NO / I DON'T KNOW

3. If so, could the relationship recover? Did you temporarily or permanently separate?

____

____

____

4. If you were cheated on, did it create a deeper wedge, or did it help identify issues and ultimately bring you closer together?

____

____

____

5. Have you ever cheated on a partner?

YES / NO

6. If yes, what led you to make that decision?

____

____

____

7. Have you ever contemplated cheating on your partner out of dissatisfaction in your relationship?

YES / NO

8. Have you personally known someone who has cheated on their partner but would never leave them?

YES / NO

9. What are your thoughts on dating/cheating sites created specifically for people in committed relationships?

____

____

____

Sexercise: Forgiveness

We are humans, and therefore, we are imperfect. Everyone makes regrettable choices that can affect others and ourselves in significant ways. If we hold on to the burden, we relive the same pain, again and again. We fixate on the injustice and allow ourselves to get caught up in self-righteousness. It's easy to justify not letting go because we feel strongly that the person doesn't deserve our forgiveness. But therein lies the problem. When we don't forgive, the only person the negative energy affects is ourselves.

The act of forgiveness is a bold act of self-love. Choosing to forgive someone, or even yourself, signifies you've come to an inner resolution to release yourself from holding onto unnecessary dead weight. When you forgive, you make the conscious decision to liberate yourself from the pain, sorrow, guilt, anger, and resentment you've carried around for too long.

In the last Sexercise of this journey, you will finally set yourself free by performing a **Forgiveness Ceremony.**

This ceremony releases the emotional baggage from any injustice that has been done to you. I feel confident almost every woman reading this guide can participate in this Sexercise, as most of us have at least one person we haven't yet forgiven for a transgression, maybe even ourselves.

Tear out a back page or two (or more) of your journal and write about your experience with the person whom you've been unable to forgive. Describe in detail the situation, filled with your emotions. This will feel painful, but you are stirring up these emotions so you may release them.

Also include why you've felt justified in not forgiving this person. If there are several people, write as many letters of forgiveness as you need to. At the end, write the following statement:

I understand this act of forgiveness is an act of self-love. Because I love myself, I will no longer allow my heart to suffer by reliving

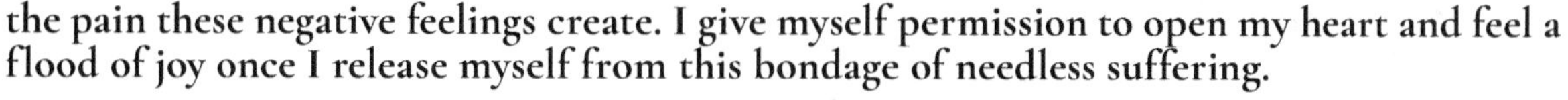

the pain these negative feelings create. I give myself permission to open my heart and feel a flood of joy once I release myself from this bondage of needless suffering.

________________ **(person's name), I forgive you. I sincerely forgive you. I can now move on with my life free from the self-created prison I've been holding myself hostage in. I understand this difficult experience has only served as a means of personal growth, and ultimately, it has strengthened me as a person.**

Take this letter (or letters) outside along with a chair, a metal bucket, and a lighter. If you don't have a metal bucket, use an outdoor fire pit or any surface that's not flammable. Now, sit in the chair and read your letter(s) aloud. When you're done, light the corner of the paper on fire and drop it into or onto the fire-safe surface. As you watch the fire devour the paper, experience the sensation of releasing all your negative emotions through the flames, and then fill your heart with feelings of forgiveness, empathy, compassion, and love. You can say a personal little prayer as well. Just feel your words deep in your heart and mean them.

Now, I have a question for you. Did you notice this Forgiveness Ceremony had nothing to do with calling or texting the person and telling them you forgive them? You can do that if you want to take this act of forgiveness a step further, but all you really need is an open heart and willingness to carry out this ceremony of forgiveness for yourself. They need not know because this act has to do with releasing *your* emotions, not theirs.

My SIM Journal

Write about your Forgiveness Ceremony if you performed one. Express how you felt while writing your forgiveness letter(s). Did it stir up negative emotions? Or did you feel a sense of surrender because you understood you were finally going to free yourself from unnecessary pain? What was the experience like for you when you set the paper on fire? Did you feel a release and allow the gentle and loving sensation of forgiveness to envelop your heart? Do you feel any desire to directly forgive this person if the person you forgave wasn't yourself? If you didn't perform a Forgiveness Ceremony, write down the reasons you feel you're not quite ready to forgive the person(s) for the pain they caused you.

* * *

If you carried out this Forgiveness Ceremony and experienced the depth of its symbolic meaning, I am very proud of you. Forgiving a person is probably one of the most difficult inner battles a person can wrestle with. Back and forth and back and forth, we go between what is right and wrong. But once you genuinely understand that forgiveness is an expression of self-love, you will feel more willing to offer forgiveness. If you're not quite ready to forgive just yet, that's okay. Take the information in this Sexercise as seeds planted. At a minimum, consider opening your heart to forgiveness.

Journey's End ... New Beginnings

Well, my friend, you made it! You've arrived at the end of your inner journey to actively improve the bond of sexual intimacy between you and your partner. Throughout your adventurous travels, you went cave diving in the deep waters of *self-exploration*. You courageously wore your open-mind hat while exploring *Fantasy Land*. You laced up your hiking boots and traversed the rugged and ever-changing terrain of *confidence*, and you went for a long swim in the vast ocean of all the reasons why ***sexual intimacy matters*** in a long-term relationship.

Throughout this guide, you've been given the opportunity to open your mind, heart, and eyes to what it really takes to rebuild a healthy and well-rounded relationship. As you've undoubtedly experienced firsthand, there are many steps in the rebuilding process. If you didn't truly value your commitment and have a sincere interest in your relationship, you would not have reached the end of this guide.

The desire to improve your relationship was set into motion through the power of intention. Your thought process was something to the effect of, "I'm not happy with the state of our relationship," or, "Things need to improve in our relationship," or, "This relationship has become lifeless, and we don't enjoy each other anymore." These thoughts of dissatisfaction formed the intention to make a positive shift in your relationship.

To make that shift happen, you sought tangible ways to help you experience a resurgence of happiness and excitement with your partner. You invested your time and energy in this guide and took actionable steps to make positive changes—a commendable action on your part.

I will leave you with three key points to help you stay focused on maintaining your new and improved relationship.

1. **USE EMPATHY.** Experience future situations from an empathetic point of view. As we all know, there are always two sides to every story, and often more. Really try to look at situations from his perspective in addition to your own and be open to see and feel his side. Ask him to reciprocate this type of understanding back to you when it's warranted.

2. **STAY FOCUSED.** When you place your focus and energy on something, you give it the best chance of success to become beautiful, flourish, and grow. Whether it's a garden, a home remodel, a business venture, or your relationship, the fruit of your labor will blossom into something of beauty, and your hard work and dedication will pay off. In the same way, when you do ***not*** nurture, tend to, or care for something, the neglect will inevitably show. Without fail, it will naturally go dormant, slow in growth, or wither and die. Therefore, remain vigilant in your focus and keep your awareness elevated on a daily basis concerning the state of your relationship.

3. **BE SELFLESS.** If you both remain devoted in your quest to frequently find ways to make each other happy, the effort you pour into one another will come back to yourselves. You will both feel special because you're mutually concentrating on pleasing each other once again.

Keep this in mind as you move forward: Everything in life is in a continuous state of change, and your relationship is no exception. As a couple, you will experience emotional closeness and distance, physical connections will increase and decrease, and bonds will strengthen and weaken. This is the natural ebb and flow of a long-term relationship. No aspect of your partnership will ever remain steady because you are two individuals going through your own growth processes and changes. But if you stay mindful about these ever-changing shifts, you will have the ability to make readjustments quickly whenever things start to slip. And don't hesitate to pull this guide off the bookshelf as a refresher to help get you back on track!

Anyone who has ever been in a long-term relationship understands they require constant attention and hard work, and they really do. *They really do.* Nope, that's not a typo. I'm repeating myself because relationships require ongoing, never-ending focus, effort, and hard work to remain fulfilling, year after year.

To me, it's such a beautiful experience and one of life's most wonderful gifts to share your life with someone you truly love. For this reason, I believe it's worth all the effort it takes to have a successful and happy relationship with the person you've chosen to spend your life with.

If you've been diligent in your efforts through this guide, and if your partner has been a willing participant, I believe you are experiencing a new and exciting version of your relationship. Now, the important part is to keep this new and improved relationship going strong. You've given yourself and your partner the special gift to genuinely enjoy each other again and to experience what it truly means to be in a healthy and loving partnership.

Now don't lose the momentum!

I sincerely wish you and your partner the absolute best and hope you have found the renewed sense of excitement, love, and desire you were seeking to reestablish in your relationship.

Continuing Sexercise Activities

Oh no...I'm not letting you off the hook that easily! You can't stop or even slow your efforts just because you've reached the end of this guide. I will leave you with some short- and long-term Sexercises for you to continue to incorporate into your relationship. Be sure to keep this list handy and refer to it often. Practice all Continuing Sexercises in the suggested time frames.

Daily

- ✓ Show three acts of affection every day.
- ✓ Say "I love you" at least once a day.
- ✓ Flirt (minimally) two times a day.
- ✓ Send him a "just because" text message. The content can be sweet, caring, loving, flirty, naughty, sexy, or suggestive, any time of the day.

Weekly

- ✓ Engage in a sexual activity twice a week but aim for more.
- ✓ Visually treat him by wearing something he loves to see on you, or something you feel confident/sexy wearing, at least once a week.
- ✓ Enjoy an in-home date night once a week.
- ✓ Partake in whatever bonding activity you've chosen as a couple.
- ✓ Show him loving and kind gestures to make him feel special and to please him.

Bi-Monthly

- ✓ Grab a drink, sit down, and converse about how you feel things are going in your relationship. Listen actively and communicate constructively with one another.
- ✓ Check your confidence level and treat yourself however you wish to keep it elevated. (Refer to CONFIDENCE IDEAS.)
- ✓ Do something special for your partner so he knows you're thinking of him. (Refer to ROMANCE/EMOTIONAL BONDING IDEAS.)
- ✓ Have a sexual communication conversation at least twice a month.

Monthly

- ✓ Go on a date night outside of the house. (Refer to DATE NIGHT IDEAS.)
- ✓ Buy at least one new outfit and/or a new piece of lingerie.
- ✓ Incorporate a sex toy into one of your sexual interactions.
- ✓ Pursue him at least once a month.

Quarterly

- ✓ Plan a roleplay once every 8 to 12 weeks. (Refer to ROLEPLAY IDEAS.)
- ✓ Read erotica, watch adult videos, or tell him a bedtime fantasy story.
- ✓ Buy or write your own card to express your feelings about him/your relationship.

Semi-Annually

- ✓ Go away on a mini vacation for a night, weekend, or long weekend.
- ✓ Book a couple's massage at a nice spa.
- ✓ Write him a love letter with a spritz of your perfume.
- ✓ Do something completely out of your norm, for example, spend the day at a nude beach. (Refer to DARE YOU CHALLENGE IDEAS.)

Annually

- ✓ Plan an adult-only vacation for one or two weeks. (Preferably two!)
- ✓ Write a list of all the things you appreciate and admire about one another and share your lists on your anniversary. Explain what makes you love each other more and more as each year passes.
- ✓ Plan a special day and night for your anniversary.

Reassess your relationship from where it was at the beginning of this journey. Do you see a significant improvement? I sincerely hope you do. Continue to journal about note-worthy events, renewed bonds, sexual exploration, and the positive changes you've made and continue to experience in your relationship.

I would love nothing more than to hear about your success stories! Email me at dearem@sexualintimacymatters.com and share with me your personal story of how your relationship has improved because of the information you've learned through this guide.

If you enjoyed this guide and would like to help spread the word, please consider leaving a book review through your purchase point.

If you are interested in receiving Sexual Intimacy Matters newsletter, The SIM Review, please visit www.sexualintimacymatters.com to sign up!

Follow me on social media! Instagram - @sexualintimacymatters, Pinterest - @sexualintimacymatters, Twitter - @dear_em71

Sexual Intimacy Ideas

Activity Bonding

- ☐ Relaxing at the beach
- ☐ Snorkeling/swimming
- ☐ Kayaking/canoeing
- ☐ Boating/fishing
- ☐ Antiquing/flea markets
- ☐ Farmers markets

- ☐ Yard/garage sales
- ☐ Woodworking
- ☐ Pottery/mosaics
- ☐ Painting/drawing
- ☐ Playing chess
- ☐ Playing cards/dominos
- ☐ Jigsaw puzzle partners
- ☐ Pool table/darts
- ☐ Binge-watch a TV series
- ☐ Traveling
- ☐ Riding motorcycles
- ☐ Skiing/snowboarding
- ☐ Mini road trips/B&Bs
- ☐ Horseback riding
- ☐ Movie night
- ☐ Date night
- ☐ Picnic in the park
- ☐ Fruit picking
- ☐ Cooking
- ☐ Theater/opera/concerts
- ☐ Dance lessons
- ☐ Couples massages
- ☐ Archery/shooting range
- ☐ Bowling
- ☐ Theme/water parks
- ☐ Volunteering
- ☐ Bird watching

- ☐ Wine tasting
- ☐ Stargazing
- ☐ Learn a new language
- ☐ House projects
- ☐ Gardening
- ☐ Board games
- ☐ Video gaming
- ☐ Work out buddies
- ☐ Hiking/biking
- ☐ Golf/tennis
- ☐ Jogging/walking

Confidence

- ☐ Take belly-dancing lessons (So much fun!)
- ☐ Perform self-affirmations every morning in the mirror
- ☐ Go lingerie shopping for sexy bras and underwear
- ☐ Purchase soft and silky sheets
- ☐ Don't compare yourself with others
- ☐ Learn something you've wanted to try but haven't
- ☐ Look in the mirror every day and say, "I love you," followed by a big self-hug
- ☐ Buy some new makeup, clothes, and shoes
- ☐ Exercise in any way, shape, or form you find enjoyable
- ☐ Take a Zumba aerobics class (My favorite exercise!)
- ☐ Try things that push your comfort zone
- ☐ What's something that makes you smile? Do that every day
- ☐ Buy a new perfume for yourself
- ☐ Shave those legs more often
- ☐ Constantly flirt with your partner
- ☐ Spend time with people who allow you to be your authentic self
- ☐ Wear something that makes you feel sexy under your clothes

Date Night ... Or Day!

- ☐ Enjoy a picnic at the beach, lake, or river
- ☐ Go to the movies
- ☐ Eat dinner at a nice restaurant
- ☐ Cook together at home and eat by candlelight
- ☐ Play billiards and darts
- ☐ Go out dancing
- ☐ Find a venue to listen to live music
- ☐ Watch a play or opera
- ☐ Get a couple's massage
- ☐ Tour botanical gardens
- ☐ Tour a brewery or bakery
- ☐ Fly kites on the beach or at a park
- ☐ Buy some ice cream cones and meander around a park
- ☐ Watch a comedy show
- ☐ Walk aimlessly around the mall and buy something new
- ☐ Go watch a professional or local sporting event
- ☐ Go see a concert

- ☐ Get a mani/pedi together
- ☐ Visit an amusement park for the day or night
- ☐ Go bowling
- ☐ Watch the sunset somewhere romantic
- ☐ Stroll around your city or town's main street and window shop
- ☐ Browse antique stores or rummage through flea markets
- ☐ Go on a dinner cruise
- ☐ Walk around a museum
- ☐ Go tubing together down a river
- ☐ Find a local festival or art show to walk around
- ☐ Go to your local farmers market on Saturday morning
- ☐ Enjoy a cup of coffee or tea at a quaint café
- ☐ Spend the night out at a hotel in another town
- ☐ Race go-karts
- ☐ Go to a VR café or arcade and play some games
- ☐ Play mini-golf or chip and putt
- ☐ Unplug and go camping
- ☐ Take a one-day class together
- ☐ Go to a sip-and-paint class
- ☐ Thrill-seekers? Go bungee jumping, skydiving, or hang gliding
- ☐ Go rock climbing indoors
- ☐ Horseback ride on a trail through the forest or along a beach
- ☐ Go to an ethnic grocery store and cook an international meal together
- ☐ Take part in a 5K walk/run together
- ☐ Rent a boat or jet skis for the day
- ☐ Go ice skating
- ☐ Walk around a zoo

- ☐ Go to a dinner theater/murder mystery show
- ☐ Go to an escape room (best to do this with other couples)
- ☐ Rent bikes and ride around a state park

Roleplay

- ☐ Boss/employee
- ☐ Masseuse/client
- ☐ Waitress/customer
- ☐ Sexy maid/customer
- ☐ Nanny/father
- ☐ Nurse/patient
- ☐ Submissive/dominatrix (female) OR submissive/dominant (male)
- ☐ Repairman/housewife
- ☐ Personal trainer/client
- ☐ Doctor/patient
- ☐ Professor/student
- ☐ Bored housewife/pool boy
- ☐ Mistress/cheating husband
- ☐ Applicant/interviewer
- ☐ Total strangers
- ☐ Escort service/client

- ☐ Stripper/customer
- ☐ Delivery guy/customer
- ☐ Police officer/perpetrator

Dare You Challenges

- ☐ During the day (if possible), make a video for him pleasuring yourself with or without a sex toy. Send it to him and tell him to watch it when he gets in the car after work.
- ☐ Meet up in a parking lot in separate cars. Get in his car and drive somewhere private so you can give him an awesome BJ.
- ☐ Spend a day in the house completely naked...all day long.
- ☐ Buy a Kama Sutra book or go online to explore different sex positions.
- ☐ Be vocal! During sex, talk dirty and make lots of sexy noises.
- ☐ Do you like to get spanked? Does he have a foot fetish? Talk about your sexual fetishes and explore them.
- ☐ Let him do a photoshoot of you posing in sexy lingerie or naked.
- ☐ Meet him outside of the house somewhere for a hookup.
- ☐ Have intoxicated, uninhibited sex.
- ☐ Tell him to purchase (by himself) a sexy outfit he'd love to see you wearing.
- ☐ Spend a day together on a nude beach.
- ☐ Find a private spot and be intimate somewhere in nature.
- ☐ Explore deeper levels of love making through tantric sex.
- ☐ Call in sick from work and spend the day in bed together reading erotica stories or

watching adult movies and have sex multiple times.

- ☐ Have a bondage encounter. Tie him up, blindfold him, and take complete advantage of him. Next time, switch roles.
- ☐ Give each other a sensual oil massage on your private parts only.
- ☐ Have sex in a different room in the house...*anywhere* but your bedroom.
- ☐ Go to an adult store together and pick out a new toy. Return home and play with it immediately!
- ☐ Wear an eye mask while having sex, or you both can wear them. This can really heighten your sense of touch.
- ☐ Play with yourselves in front of each other, all the way to orgasm.
- ☐ Give him a sexy striptease and lap-dance.
- ☐ Give him a completely hands-free BJ.
- ☐ Have a sweet tooth? Buy liquid chocolate or whip cream to add a little flavor to oral sex.
- ☐ When you take your next road trip, start talking about anything sex-related that will create a sexual buildup. When you can no longer handle the anticipation, stop at the next rest area, find a parking spot far away from other cars/people, and have passionate sex in the back seat.
- ☐ Spend the night at a hotel and pack all your sex toys in your suitcase along with some sexy wear. Enjoy a night filled with lots of sexual fun.
- ☐ Go to a body of water where you can find a private spot to skinny dip.
- ☐ Drive separately to a local bar. Order a drink and then go sit or stand next to him and act like your strangers meeting for the first time. Casually talk about your lives and steer the conversation in the direction that you're interested in hooking up with him. Take him back to "your house" and have a crazy, passionate sexual encounter as "strangers."
- ☐ When you spend the night in a hotel, go into the bathroom and change into a sexy maid outfit and pretend to be the housekeeping service. Flirt with him and tease him and then seduce him into having sex while his 'wife' left to get a spa treatment.

Romance & Emotional Bonding

- ☐ Take a sensual, candlelit bubble bath together.
- ☐ Grab a bottle of wine and a blanket, and head to a quiet and private place to stargaze.
- ☐ Lounge around a pool together, both in and out of the water.
- ☐ Fill your bedroom with lots of tealight candles before you have sex.
- ☐ Get a couple Starbucks drinks and go sit and talk on a park bench, day or night.
- ☐ Take a blanket to a park and find a spot you can lie under a tree canopy to hang out and spend time together.
- ☐ Leave him a love note in his car or on a napkin you packed in his lunch.
- ☐ Buy a glass jar and fill it with his favorite treats. Keep refilling!
- ☐ Sit outside or indoors by a warm fire together and snuggle up.
- ☐ Get a couple's massage.
- ☐ While he's taking a shower, draw a big heart on a steamy bathroom mirror for him to find when he gets out.
- ☐ Give each other foot rubs or shoulder massages after a long day of work.
- ☐ Make a nice breakfast and bring it to him in bed.
- ☐ Buy a single balloon that says "I love you" or "You're special" and tie it to the back

of his office or kitchen chair.

- ☐ Make a short, 3-bullet list of what you love the most about him. Put it on his nightstand for him to find.
- ☐ Make his favorite lunchtime meal and bring it to his work. If you don't have time because you work, order lunch from his favorite restaurant and have it delivered to his work.
- ☐ Together, plan a getaway to escape your routine for a minimum of 24 hours.
- ☐ On the drive to your getaway, play "our song" and tell him how much he still means to you after all these years.
- ☐ Spend an evening unplugged and play your favorite board games accompanied by your favorite (alcoholic or non-alcoholic) drinks.
- ☐ Buy a special candle on your anniversary, and at the end of the night, light the candle and set it between the two of you. Tell each other how grateful you feel to be spending your lives together and share what you look forward to as a couple in the coming year.

***

I hope you will take the time and thoroughly enjoy every one of these ideas with your partner. Get your creative juices flowing and incorporate some of your own ideas too! Engaging in these activities will keep your sexual intimacy bond and your relationship solid, strong, and filled with never-ending gestures of love and interest for each other.

Resources:

https://www.psychologytoday.com/us
https://www.onhealth.com/script/main/hp.asp
https://www.thebabbleout.com/
https://www.therecoveryvillage.com/

In Loving Memory of My Sweet Silvi

Your passion and zeal for life were contagious and something I truly admired about you. I will always remember your beautiful smile, your amazing energy, and your unwavering kindness.

May your spirit forever dance in the wind, just like the butterflies you so adored. Though our life paths crossed for only a brief moment in time, your precious soul is one I will never forget.

1983 - 2018

www.ingramcontent.com/pod-product-compliance
Lightning Source LLC
LaVergne TN
LVHW061222100826
845148LV00004B/825

* 9 7 8 1 7 3 6 5 6 1 5 1 5 *